SILENT
NO MORE

HOW I BECAME A POLITICAL PRISONER OF MUELLER'S *"WITCH HUNT"*

JEROME R. CORSI, Ph.D.

Post Hill
PRESS

A POST HILL PRESS BOOK
ISBN: 978-1-64293-217-1
ISBN (eBook): 978-1-64293-218-8

Silent No More:
How I Became a Political Prisoner of Mueller's "Witch Hunt"
© 2019 by Jerome R. Corsi, Ph.D.
All Rights Reserved

Cover art by Cody Corcoran

Post Hill Press
New York • Nashville
posthillpress.com

Published in the United States of America

Dedicated to:

President Donald J. Trump,
with whom I have had a cordial and
very respectful relation
over many years.

Jim Garrow,
whose advice has proved invaluable My Loving Family,
from whom Mueller & Co.
have threatened to separate me.

And
The Volunteer Staff of CorsiNation.com,
whose dedication to God and to the Constitution
continue to inspire me.

"No one who had once fallen into the hands of the Thought Police ever escaped in the end. They were corpses waiting to be sent to the grave."

—*George Orwell,* 1984

"But the Lord is with me as a mighty terrible one: therefore my persecutors shall stumble, and they shall not prevail: they shall be greatly ashamed; for they shall not prosper: their everlasting confusion shall never be forgotten."

—*Jeremiah 20:11*

CONTENTS

My Kafkaesque Nightmare

Now, AS I write this in my senior years, I find myself threatened with imprisonment for the first time in my life. With the confusion and frustration that prevailed over the Robert Mueller prosecutors after two months of trying to cooperate with them, I anticipate now I may be sentenced so severely for one crime or another that I will die in prison, all because of the way Robert Mueller's "witch hunt" prosecution operates.

My Kafkaesque nightmare began by spending the last two months—September and October 2018—being mentally tortured by Mueller's Deep State prosecutors, while being held incommunicado with my cellphone and laptop confiscated. So being isolated, one step short of being incarcerated. I was interrogated for up to eight hours at a stretch in six sessions over the two months in question, all occurring within a windowless conference room deep within the bowels of an unmarked FBI building in southeast Washington, D.C.

Every night now I am plagued by the most terror-inspiring dreams of finding myself going insane in solitary confinement—something I know the Deep State monsters would enjoy. From the moment my last book, *Killing the Deep State: The Fight to Save President Trump*, became a *New York Times* bestseller, I knew the totalitarian masters of the Deep State minions had targeted me to be censored, silenced, and ultimately incarcerated.

The pages of this book should warn all readers that the United States under the Deep State masters has begun to descend into a political hell that I previously thought could only happen under Hitler's

Gestapo, Stalin's KGB, or Mao's Cultural Revolution. My particular Kafkaesque nightmare is nothing more than punishment for the crime of being a vocal supporter of Donald Trump and for having worked with Roger Stone to promote Trump's 2016 presidential campaign. Had I supported Hillary Clinton, I would today be a Deep State role model and hero.

My "crimes" against the Deep State are compounded by the twenty books I have authored or co-authored since 2004—first joining the Swift Boat movement against John Kerry, followed by exposing Barack Obama as a radical socialist with intellectual roots in communism and a history of being a cultural Muslim since his childhood. My book exposing Obama's birth certificate fraud earned me from the Hard Left the permanent slander of being dismissed as a "conspiracy theorist."

As my attorney David Gray said to me in the midst of this experience, "You have to look back and realize there are a lot of Democratic Party corpses in your wake."

In reading the pages that follow, I have only one request: Please understand the nightmare I am now experiencing could and most likely will happen to you or someone near to you if you do not stand up and oppose the Deep State. In the Deep State dystopia being planned by the hard left, there will be no freedom left for those who dare express allegiance to the flag of the United States and the constitutional freedoms bequeathed all Americans by our founding fathers. This will be especially true if that allegiance is compounded by a Judeo-Christian belief in God or more particularly, a decision to accept Jesus Christ as your personal savior.

November 5, 2018

New Jersey

CHAPTER 1

It Begins

It was Tuesday, August 28, 2018, three days before my seventy-second birthday, when the doorbell rang at our home in a wooded area of northern New Jersey at approximately 3:30 PM.

My wife, Monica, and I were in my study discussing family financing. Since 2016, I had lost several lucrative consulting jobs I had in Washington, D.C., including InfoWars, where I had been working as Washington Bureau Chief since shortly after Donald Trump's inauguration.

Since the election of Donald Trump as president, the hard left has targeted InfoWars as the spearhead to attack economically. The goal was to force InfoWars and all reporters associated with Alex Jones off the internet. The intent was to punish economically and silence all conservative and libertarian critics of the hard left's increasingly aggressive socialist goals. Not stopping at imposing political censorship through social media giants including Google, YouTube, Facebook, and Twitter, the hard left also threatened corporate clients who hired as consultants so-called "conspiracy theorists" such as me.

In the ensuing two years since the 2016 surprise election of President Trump, the hard left has intensified into a violent "resist and obstruct" movement designed ultimately to use the criminal investigation of Robert Mueller's Special Counsel office as a means of criminalizing politics. The ultimate goal of the hard left is to first impeach, then imprison Donald Trump through utterly false charges the Trump campaign colluded with Russia to steal the presidency from Hillary Clinton.

When I asked over the intercom who was at the front door, the answer came back, "The FBI."

That was a frightening moment for both me and Monica. Truthfully, finding the FBI at the front door was not entirely unexpected. The press had been reporting for weeks that the Mueller investigation was systematically questioning all associates of well-known political activist Roger Stone. Clearly, I had to be on the list.

In February 2016, I met Roger Stone for the first time, but within a few weeks, I began playing a double-role of being both a reporter and a political operative.

I reported on Stone's political activities to advise Donald Trump during the 2016 presidential campaign. My job at that time was to work as a full-time reporter for World Net Daily, WND.com. I held this job since 2004 when Joseph Farah, founder and CEO of WND.com, asked me to join him. In that year, I had co-authored with John O'Neill my first number one run-away bestseller. The book entitled *Unfit for Command: Swift Boat Veterans Speak Out Against John Kerry* became known as the "Swift Boat book."

With *Unfit for Command*, we coined "Swift Boating" as a new term in politics. The hard left, of course, used the term derogatively, suggesting a "Swift Boat" attack involved destroying a political candidate by lies and smears. That book that is widely credited with derailing John Kerry's 2004 presidential aspirations, and I will stand by the truth of every word.

At the same time, I had crossed over from the reporter's role to work behind the scenes as a political operative, working secretly with Roger Stone to engineer events that would affect the news cycle favorably for the Trump campaign during the 2016 presidential election. Joseph Farah had long established the policy at WND.com that as reporters we were encouraged not to mask our political leanings. Instead, reporters at WND were also encouraged to publish opinion pieces as commentary.

When the doorbell rang, I could see my wife was shaken by the news that the FBI was at the doorstep. "Here we go again," Monica said. She had long been afraid my writing on the political right would land me in prison. Her fears and mine intensified as Deep State moved to convert the federal government into an Orwellian surveillance state where people could be punished or executed for their political views. I began to have this worry when the IRS began a series of costly audits of my tax returns in 2004—a move I believe the Deep State took to retaliate against me for my role in co-authoring *Unfit for Command* and assisting with the Swift Boat movement against John Kerry.

In 1991, I married Monica, some ten years my junior, three months after first meeting her in New Jersey. Before meeting Monica, I had resolved never again to be married. I fell in love with Monica the first time I saw her. I have often joked that the reason I asked Monica to marry me some three months after I met her was that I knew I had to marry this woman before she had time to learn too much about me. My whole life story has had so many unexpected twists and turns that I doubt anyone, including myself, will ever fully comprehend it.

Monica was born in La Plata, Argentina to parents born in Italy. She is a beautiful woman with flowing blonde hair and a sharp temper. One of her great strengths is that as quickly as she can flare in anger, she can forgive. But from the beginning, I knew marrying Monica was the wrong woman to choose if I had any aspirations to be unfaithful to her. That was one transgression she would never forgive.

Prior to living in New Jersey, I had spent some fifteen years living in the western United States, first moving to Albuquerque, New Mexico in 1976, where I had a position as a research professor at the University of New Mexico, first in the Political Science Department and subsequently in the Department of Public Administration. In Denver, Colorado, I changed careers after deciding I could never truly succeed in an academic environment that was beginning to be dominated by leftists.

In Denver, I began my career in bank marketing. I subsequently moved to Portland, Oregon, where I helped a fledgling company, Marketing One, develop into a national company that sold a billion dollars a year in annuities through banks, plus another billion dollars in mutual funds. In 1990, I had been living in White Plains, New York, where I was working for yet another bank marketing company. This one was called Independent Financial Marketing Group, a company whose founder hailed from South Africa. In 1990, I came to Morris Plains, New Jersey, where I was recruited by a national bank marketing firm headquartered on Route 10 off Interstate 287. My job there was to develop a securities mutual fund sales program to accompany the annuity marketing the firm had been implementing for years. That's where I met Monica.

When I married Monica, she was aware of my political interests—I had received a Ph.D. from the Political Science Department at Harvard in 1972, when I was twenty-five years old. She knew me when we first got married as a financial services expert who worked with banks in the United States as well as overseas to implement bank marketing programs through which the banks sold insurance and securities products to their retail customers—activities that since the Depression, the Glass-Steagall Act had been largely forbidden for commercial banks to do.

The truth is that I had been involved in presidential politics since I was a child. Throughout my childhood, my father worked in downtown Cleveland, Ohio, where he was employed by the Brotherhood of Railroad Trainmen, first as the Assistant Editor of the union's newspaper, the *Trainmen News*, then as the union's first Director of Public Relations. On January 1, 1969, my father's crowning career achievement was realized when the United Transportation Union (UTU) was born. With the personal assistance of President Lyndon Johnson and the advice of Edward Bernays, commonly considered the father of public relations, my father managed to engineer the creation of the UTU by combining what were then known as the five railroad operating unions. Since the early 1950s, my father played a role in Democratic Party politics, representing the union.

As a child, I was a truant from kindergarten who refused to attend elementary school. I preferred to stay home to watch the televised organized crime hearings chaired by the slow-talking Democratic Senator from Tennessee, Estes Kefauver, after the creation of the United States Special Committee to Investigate Crime. I distinctly remember watching on television with my father the 1952 Republican National Convention in Chicago that nominated popular war hero Dwight D. Eisenhower of Kansas for president, followed by the Democratic National Convention also held in Chicago that year. In 1952, the Democrats nominated for president Illinois Governor Adlai E. Stevenson.

I spent considerable time with my father in Washington, watching such historic events as the McClellan Committee. In 1957, the McClellan Committee's investigation of organized crime moving into the Teamsters Union helped launch Jack Kennedy's presidential career. I learned politics spending hours in the Senate gallery in the hours when my father had business dealings with the government on behalf of the union.

In 2004, when John Kerry began emerging as the likely Democratic Party presidential candidate, I decided it was time for me to re-enter the political arena. I went up to the attic of our home and brought down a box of old papers, explaining to Monica that I was going to do my best to block Kerry from the White House.

"Who are you to do this?" Monica asked incredulously.

That led to a long discussion where I had to disclose to Monica that as an undergraduate at Case Western Reserve University (CWRU) in Cleveland, I had worked with the CWRU Civil Violence Research Center. Subsequently, as a graduate student at Harvard, I did contract work for the Lemberg Center for the Study of Violence at Brandeis University—a nationally renowned research institute headed by the renown psychiatrist John Spiegel of the Spiegel catalogue family fame.

Always in these jobs I was working under a government contract in work that first brought me into contact with various law enforcement and intelligence agencies, including the FBI and the CIA.

In the early 1970s, I worked in a Lemberg Center project under contract with the then Law Enforcement Assistance Administration (LEAA), a federal agency that was established under the Omnibus Crime Control and Safe Streets Act of 1968. The LEAA at that time was part of the U.S. Department of Justice. One of my assignments was to work undercover with the FBI to penetrate the Vietnam Veterans Against the War (VVAW), a vocal organization of anti-war activists whose public figurehead at the time was none other than John Kerry.

In the course of that assignment, we established that Kerry, while he was yet in the Naval Reserves, had met in Paris as a representative of the VVAW with the beautiful, politically sophisticated Madame Nguyễn Thị Bình, who at that time was the chief negotiator to the Paris peace talks for the Viet Cong. Informing Naval Intelligence of the discovery, undercover U.S. intel operatives photographed Kerry in Paris wearing his Navy uniform going to meetings with Madame Bình. This violation of the military code, and possibly of U.S. law, resulted in John Kerry getting a "less than honorable" discharge from the Navy—a disgrace that later blocked Kerry from being accepted at the Harvard Law School.

Over the years, including while reporting for WND.com, I have had continued experience working with the FBI to report on various aspects of criminal activity. In recent years, at the invitation of the FBI, I was the sole reporter allowed to attend in El Salvador a DOJ-sponsored conference on criminal Hispanic gangs. That conference highlighted the FBI's work internationally with countries in Mexico as well as Central and South America where the violent El Salvadorian-based gang MS-13 is a menace.

In our twenty-seven-year marriage, Monica and I had managed through many very difficult times. I had come to learn that with

Monica, I had a marriage partner I could rely upon to be a mature-thinking pillar of strength through what was certain to be one of the greatest tests we were forced to face together. In the years after 2004, the IRS had also showed up at our doorstep, demanding to interrogate me about my tax filings. Monica's analysis in difficult times, including now, often has included advice that I did not want to hear. But I have also come to realize that Monica's perspective is so important that I had to listen. Today, with the Mueller Special Counsel criminal investigation, we were going to have to navigate through what now was developing to be the most difficult challenge of our marriage.

Once the FBI announced their presence at the front door, our next move would be to contact our attorney. Anything I said to the FBI from that moment on would be reported, with the risk that it is a federal felony to lie to the FBI. With the possibility I could go to federal prison for anything I said to the FBI from that moment on, I resolved not to talk with the agents at the door, but to thank them politely and send them away, letting them know my attorney would speak promptly with the Department of Justice official to whom they were reporting.

The first problem was that our four-month-old German Shepherd had responded to the doorbell with predictable loud and angry barking. Lobo, a Spanish name that means "wolf," was acting as if he could just savor taking several bites out of the hides of the two FBI agents who had just rang the doorbell.

As Monica subdued Lobo and got him into the basement, I opened the door to greet the two FBI agents. Both were young and very professional, neatly groomed and sharply dressed in coats and ties.

The two agents introduced themselves, showing me their identification. Agents Smith and Agent Jones (both obvious pseudonyms designed to protect the identity of two FBI agents at the door) then presented me with a two-page subpoena to appear ten days later, on

Friday, September 7, 2018, in Washington, D.C., to testify before the Mueller grand jury.

Monica, who joined me at the front door, scanned with me the two-page subpoena.

The agents, who were clearly anxious to be invited inside to begin questioning me, were blocked when I said quietly, "I will immediately contact my attorney and he will be in touch with you right away." The agents backed off and explained that the contact person in Washington who had issued the subpoena was Aaron Zelinsky.

Zelinsky was a forty-two-year-old professional prosecutor before joining Mueller's Special Counselor team who had worked in the office of the U.S. Attorney in the District of Maryland as an Assistant U.S. Attorney under current Deputy Attorney General Rod Rosenstein, who was then overseeing for the Department of Justice the U.S. Attorneys in the District of Maryland.[1] Zelinsky graduated from Hopkins, a preparatory school located in New Haven, Connecticut, in 2002, having served as president of the student council. He went on to receive a Bachelor of Arts in Economics from Yale College in 2006 and a Doctor of Jurisprudence (JD, DOJ) from Yale Law School in 2010.

I knew Zelinsky had a distinguished career in the Department of Justice in Richmond, Virginia, where he had earned an award for excellence in the prosecution of organized crime. In 2012, Zelinsky served as a legal advisor in the Obama State Department. Following that, Zelinsky clerked for Judge Thomas Griffith, a George W. Bush appointee on the D.C. Circuit Court of Appeals. In 2013, Zelinsky clerked for now-retired justices John Paul Stevens and Anthony Kennedy on the Supreme Court. His resumé even included a stint

---

1   Hosenball, Alex; Thomas, Pierre; Levine, Mike; and Goetz, Dylan. "Meet special counselor Robert Mueller's prosecution team," ABC News, May 17, 2018. *https://abcnews.go.com/Politics/ meet-special-counsel-robert-muellers-prosecution-team/story?id=55219043.*

serving for three months in 2012 as an adjunct professor at the Peking University School of Transitional Law in Shenzhen, China, followed by serving as a visiting assistant professor of law at the University of Maryland's law school in Baltimore.

Put simply, I recognized Zelinsky as an experienced, hardworking, brilliant up-and-coming DOJ career prosecutor who was a force that we had to take very seriously. As I determined from the moment the FBI announced their presence, I was determined to be questioned by the FBI at the door. I fully appreciated lying to the FBI was a federal criminal felony, and I knew how easily the well-trained FBI field personnel armed with a subpoena could develop a perjury trap by questioning inexperienced people. Those frightened by a subpoena are often tempted to explain their way out of a difficult situation by attempting to justify their behavior to the FBI field agents delivering the subpoena. This is almost always a costly mistake.

I had no intention of talking to the FBI without the advice and presence of my attorney, David Gray. But my problem was that 2016 was two years past and I knew my memory was less than perfect, more than capable of playing tricks on me.

I immediately assumed FBI Agents Smith and Jones were operating under a special assignment to Mueller's special counselor team in Washington. My guess was these two agents had travelled from Washington specifically to deliver the subpoena to me at my New Jersey home. My guess was that they would report back to Zelinsky and that I would see them again, in the FBI interrogation room in Washington.

Agents Smith and Jones acted very professionally and politely, a trademark of FBI agents in the field. In return, I aimed to be equally calm, polite, and professional in my responses to them at the front door.

"Thank you, gentlemen," I assured the FBI agents. "Please let Mr. Zelinsky know that my attorney will be in touch with him as soon as I have a chance to confer with my attorney."

Agents Smith and Jones accepted that response, we thanked each other, and they departed quietly.

Much later, I learned Agents Smith and Jones had been frightened at Lobo's barking. "That sounded like one big dog," Agent Smith later told us, driving my attorney, David Gray, and me from the Mayflower Hotel in Washington to the federal courthouse in southeast D.C., to appear before the Mueller grand jury.

Listening to the dog at the door, Agents Smith and Jones went instantly on alert, ready to pull their service side-arm weapons in self-defense. From experience, FBI agents delivering subpoenas know that the angry barks of a large dog can quickly turn into a vicious and life-threatening dog attack once the door is open. Few Americans realize how many dogs the FBI is forced to shoot and kill in similar door-knocks to protect themselves from angry dogs doing their job.

Once the FBI agents departed, I turned to Monica and said, "Let's call David Gray."

We both knew that I had just entered a national FBI criminal investigation being conducted at the highest and most visible political level in our nation's history.

I suspected immediately the target of the investigation for which I was being summoned was Roger Stone and that my testimony was required to help Mueller's prosecutors build their criminal case to convict Roger Stone of a criminal felony and to squeeze him to turn state's evidence against Donald Trump.

Still, that day I knew the outcome could easily be that I would be imprisoned as a felon even if Mueller had subpoenaed me to be a witness, not as a target, if I had a lapse of memory or made a misstep in testimony before Mueller's Special Counsel and the FBI.

Even with the advice of David Gray, I was not sure I could avoid a perjury trap even though I fully intended to tell the truth. From what I knew of the manner, FBI investigators and Department of Justice prosecutors were capable of playing the perjury trap game, I felt scared. In the pit of my stomach, this was a game that was set up, so I could lose, even if I felt certain I was telling the truth.

CHAPTER 2

Enter David Gray

THE NEXT DAY, Wednesday, August 29, 2018, our attorney, David Gray, came to our home to conference with me and Monica. We needed to develop a strategy to respond to the Mueller subpoena.

David Gray is an imposing but soft-spoken six-foot five-inch native of New Jersey who graduated from Rutgers University with a Bachelor of Science degree in Organizational Management, and from Seton Hall University School of Law in 2003 with his JD degree. David sports a trendy, neatly trimmed short beard and he wears eyeglasses that dominate much of his face, framing his hazel eyes.

Before the Mueller subpoena, David had already served as attorney for Monica and me for some time, having been recommended by our accountant Michael Loffredo. Both Michael Loffredo and David Gray are local practitioners owning and managing their own small professional firms. Monica had worked with Michael Loffredo's father since before we were married. Throughout our marriage, we have used the same accountants and the same lawyers.

For some thirty-five years, Monica has owned and managed a large, well-respected cleaning and maintenance company named MoniMel, Inc., that Monica had started with her mother, Melania. Michael Loffredo and his father before him had worked with Monica and me to manage our finances, aware that the IRS was politically motivated and could be watching at any time.

Monica is "general secretary and treasurer" of the Corsi family, managing all our money. She and her advisers Michael Loffredo and David Gray are meticulous, making sure every penny received and spent is accounted for, properly entered into the banking system with full income reported to the IRS and to the New Jersey tax authorities, with all required taxes paid.

Now, on Wednesday, August 29, 2018, it was going to be David Gray's opportunity to manage us through a more challenging and potentially perilous encounter with the FBI and Robert Mueller's Special Counsel office that was certain to draw national, if not international, coverage. At stake, ultimately in the outcome, was not only my freedom, but the future of the Trump presidency. Mueller's target, in my case, might have been Roger Stone, but none of us had any doubt that Roger Stone for Mueller was just an intermediary case necessary to establish that the Trump campaign had colluded with Russia to steal the 2016 presidential election from Hillary Clinton.

Curiously, Tom Bergeron, a Whippany-based reporter for the business newspaper *ROI-NJ*, became intrigued that David Gray, whose office is in a three-story brick building at the intersection of Route 10 and 287 in Whippany, would be chosen as a "small-town New Jersey lawyer" to represent a key figure in the Mueller probe.[2]

"Last Thursday night, David Gray squeezed his 6-foot 5-inch frame into the tiny chairs that make up a second-grade classroom during Back to School Night at the elementary school his kids attend," Bergeron wrote. "On Friday, he went to the law office that bears his name on Route 10 West in Whippany and did work on a real estate transaction (a restaurant in Morris Plains is being sold), a divorce case (surprise, surprise: something came up there) and an employment case relating to the departure of a bank president. On Monday

2   Bergeron, Tom. "Small-town N.J. lawyer confident as he heads to D.C. to represent key figure in Mueller probe," ROI New Jersey, September 16, 2018. *http://www.roi-nj.com/2018/09/16/law/ big-day-for-small-town-n-j-lawyer-david-gray-is-confident-as-he-heads-to-d-c-to-represent-key-figure-in-mueller-probe/*.

morning, he'll be in Washington, D.C., handling the defense of a client who has been subpoenaed in the Mueller investigation."

Bergeron puzzled that David Gray, the head of a three-attorney law practice, the Gray Law Group, that does most of its work representing families and small businesses in New Jersey, would get picked for this assignment. "I have a duty to my client to say if I feel I'm not the right person to represent them, to refer them to the right person," Gray explained to the New Jersey business journal. "I've had some very honest discussions with Dr. Corsi and his family about that. And I've got to tell you: I am 100 percent convinced, as is Dr. Corsi and his family, that I am the right person for it."

On Wednesday, August 29, 2018, David was settled with Monica at the long table of our family room.

As David studied the Mueller subpoena, he validated for Monica and me that the subpoena required me to appear before the Special Counsel's grand jury in Washington, D.C., on Friday, September 7, 2018. If I failed to appear, I could be charged with a criminal offense and if I lied before the grand jury, I was certain to serve time in a federal penitentiary, branded for life as a federal felon.

"This is a serious matter," David explained, "and we have to take it very seriously." David waited until after we had spoken before he contacted prosecutor Aaron Zelinsky in Mueller's Special Counselor office. David was surprised the subpoena had been served precisely ten days prior to my appearance before the Mueller grand jury was required—the minimum time allowed by statute for the serving of that subpoena.

This implied that the Mueller prosecutors had been planning for some time to call me before the Mueller grand jury, but they waited until they were ready to do so. From this, David speculated that we might have the final pieces the Mueller prosecutors needed to develop their case against Roger Stone—the person David agreed was likely the target of this part of the Mueller investigation.

David insisted that even if the FBI wanted me as a witness, we had to develop carefully a strategy regarding how we were going to respond. "By the steps we take now," David insisted, "we have to improve our chances that you will be a witness and that you will come out of this without inadvertently becoming a victim."

Since the moment FBI door-knock the day before, I, too, knew we needed to develop a strategy before I said a word to the FBI. I had been considering whether we improved our chances of a favorable outcome by cooperating with the Mueller investigation.

"Isn't it true that Zelinsky could get a search warrant and have the FBI show up at dawn, fully armed, with a SWAT team, ready to break down the door to search the house and take whatever they want?" I asked.

"Yes," David said, although he cautioned the FBI could have already done that, if the Special Prosecutor had so instructed.

This idea frightened Monica, but I thought it was best to get that possibility off the table right away.

"Then why don't we just offer to give them everything that they might otherwise get a search warrant to seize," I asked. The strategy I had been developing overnight was that we should cooperate with the Mueller investigation, making it easy for them to obtain what they needed to pursue their investigation. Besides, given the extensive investigative powers available to the Special Prosecutor and the Department of Justice, I suspected the FBI already had everything we might decide to turn over voluntarily.

In 2011, preparing for the 2012 presidential campaign cycle, I had purchased a seventeen-inch MacBook Pro laptop that I continued to use into 2017. That laptop took a lot of nursing to keep it going. At one time, the motherboard, termed by Apple to be a "Logic Board," failed. Apple replaced the 2011 motherboard with a free upgrade and we had just made the expiration of the "free replacement" offer by a few days. At another time, the keyboard quit functioning. For a MacBook Pro, the replacement of the keyboard required replacing the entire computer casing. Over time, we had upgraded the hard disk to a solid-state hard disk, while increasing the RAM (Random Access Memory) to the maximum.

I had worked hard to salvage the seventeen-inch laptop as long as possible because Apple had discontinued making a seventeen-inch laptop shortly after I bought mine in 2011. Fortunately, I had used an external hard-disk storage device to house the Time Machine backups. This meant I could hand over to the FBI the computer I had used during the 2016 presidential campaign, along with a Time Machine backup device that had stored the contents of the laptop four times a month. Or if there was a way to alter the Time Machine backups, it was beyond my technical computer competence to know how to do so.

The best thing about the Time Machine backup was that I could restore the laptop to any given past backup date and there was no way I could go back and alter the backups. Once stored, the backups were locked into the Time Machine such that they constituted a permanent, non-changeable record of my computer during the period the FBI wanted to investigate. Handing over the seventeen-inch laptop plus the Time Machine backup device would constitute full transparency to the FBI, indicating that I had nothing to hide.

Additionally, I had a thirteen-inch MacBook Air that I began using when the seventeen-inch laptop failed, and an iPhone 8 Plus cellphone that I was also willing to hand over. I also proposed to David and Monica that I would offer to sign consent forms, so the FBI could directly search all my email and other internet accounts that the FBI might consider relevant. Why not do so, since I figured the FBI already had or could easily obtain all this data anyway, with the possible exception of the data in the Time Machine backup device?

"Are you sure there is nothing on you in those devices that could constitute evidence of a crime?" David asked, warning us the Department of Justice could prosecute me for any crime that was evidenced on those devices, even if the crime the FBI detected was unrelated to the Mueller investigation. This precipitated a discussion that we had been scrupulous with full reporting to the IRS and complete payment of all taxes due since the first IRS audit tracing back to 2004. We had no foreign bank accounts and we avoided cash transactions, so all our income and expenses could be fully accounted for and reported.

As far as I could recall, there was a lot of information, including information on those devices about my outside consulting activities. But that information would probably not be interesting to the prosecutors, since my outside consulting work was not the subject of their investigation and I always made certain my outside consulting work did not involve anything remotely related to criminal activity.

Still, I knew that by handing over these devices to the Department of Justice my life since 2012 would be an open book. Making the decision to hand over all my electronic devices, all my email accounts, and everything trackable about me on the internet, I realized was about to enter a first hand experience of the power of the totalitarian state we are entering in the United States, where there is about to be no such thing as a private conversation or a confidential email.

David explained that what I was proposing was in legal terms considered a "proffer"—an agreement between federal prosecutors and someone under criminal investigation that allows the suspect to give the government information about crimes in return for some assurances the individuals involved would be protected against prosecution.[3]

"There is no assurance we will get immunity by offering to hand over to the FBI everything the FBI wants to see," David cautioned. "But the move is certain to be received favorably by the Mueller prosecutors and will most likely improve our chances." David too had reviewed Zelinsky's background and knew we were facing a formidable adversary who was certain to be well-prepared.

David also warned us that we were facing what he termed the "perjury trap."

---

3   "Proffer Agreement Law and Legal Definition," USLegal.com. *https://definitions.uslegal.com/p/proffer-agreement.*

In recent years, the FBI has become adept at trapping witnesses into a "perjury trap." The technique involves the unfair advantage the FBI has obtaining via search warrants all relevant investigative information about a suspect before the person is interviewed. Even if a person is resolved to tell the truth to the FBI, human memory is fallible. A person who makes a definitive statement is at risk if the FBI has any evidence that can demonstrate that statement is not 100 percent accurate.

So, a response, "I never met that person," could put a suspect in jeopardy of perjury, provided the FBI has evidence to the contrary. Most people find it difficult to couch every answer with a qualification. "To the best of my recollection, I do not remember meeting that person," is a much safer answer. The qualification does not exclude the possibility the suspect responding may have met the person but forgot. Still, systematic forgetting in responding to the FBI is still a crime if the "forgetting" is intentional in order to protect a possible target of the investigation, or to otherwise frame a response that in reality is not truthful.

"By volunteering to cooperate," David advised, "we make it more difficult for the FBI to prosecute you in a perjury trap. If you are offering to hand over all available information relevant to the FBI's investigation, the FBI will have a much harder time establishing at a criminal trial that your response proved you were intending to lie."

We also discussed with David if he was the best choice to represent us. Typically, someone who is subpoenaed in a high-profile federal criminal investigation would seek to obtain legal representation from a top New York or Washington-based nationally recognized law firm.

This was a point reporter Tom Bergeron discussed.

"Of all the twists and turns and drama associated with Robert Mueller's investigation, this may be the hardest to believe: The lawyer for Jerry Corsi—an investigative journalist and/or conspiracy theorist who has written bestselling books, worked for InfoWars and is being subpoenaed to discuss his relationship with former Donald

Trump adviser Roger Stone—works in an eight-person office where the phone often is answered by Gray's wife, Ivana," Bergeron wrote.

David Gray was aware of the high-profile nature of the case.

"Corsi has a long history of writings connected to presidential politics," Gray acknowledged to Bergeron. "He is the guy who came up with the swift boat conspiracy involving John Kerry, which jammed him up. He's the one who came up with the birther issue on President Barack Obama and jammed him up."

Gray continued: "Corsi tried to do everything he could to help Donald Trump get elected and, in the middle of that campaign, he had a lot of back and forth with a guy named Roger Stone, who was with the Trump campaign—and there was a lot of discussion of back and forth involving WikiLeaks and Julian Assange. That's what this is about."

Gray also explained to the journalist that he feels he has a 100 percent duty to all his clients, requiring him to tell a client outright if Gray feels he is not the right person to take the case.

"I've had some very honest discussions with Dr. Corsi and his family about that," Gray continued in his explanation to Bergeron. "And I've got to tell you: I am 100 percent convinced, as is Dr. Corsi and his family, that I am the right person for it."

This was correct, as evidenced by the discussion we were having the day after I got the Mueller subpoena. From my own experience, I knew that hiring a big-name law firm might not be the solution. Yes, my case was likely to be a high-profile case that many big-name firms would be happy to take on.

From prior experience, a major problem with high-profile laws firms was that after paying retainer fees that are typically excessive, a junior lawyer at the firm would get assigned to do the all-important grunt work for partners distracted by better paying assignments.

What I know from my own reporting is that most of the work, if the job is done right, is grunt work. That's why I do my own research and reporting. My staff consists of me—nobody else. I feel more than competent to do what is needed to produce news reporting and analysis that will command national and international attention, even if it takes an enormous amount of time to research each article and book I author.

Besides, I felt David was determined to be fully prepared and I knew he appreciated the skill of the federal prosecutors we were about to face.

"Mueller's prosecutors are not good attorneys, they're great attorneys," Gray told Bergeron. "They are extraordinarily bright. They are probably the best of the best.

Gray elaborated: "Here's where I see their smarts as a lawyer. They are extraordinarily prepared. And they are very strategic on getting information and what they disclose. They are so well-prepared, they don't miss a beat."

David's interview with Bergeron confirmed my own conclusions.

"It's heavy lifting, yes," he said. "But it's certainly not outside the scope of what we can handle. "There's only a handful of lawyers who are going to have some contact with Mueller's investigation one way or another. I don't think you have to be a high-powered D.C. lawyer to be one of those lawyers."

Gray explained the situation to Bergeron accurately and precisely.

"I have no doubt in my mind that there are high-powered D.C. lawyers who would be champing at the bit to represent Doctor Corsi," Gray told the reporter. "There's only a handful of lawyers in the world who are involved in the Mueller investigation."

But the bottom line is that Gray has always understood the law is the law.

"On the one hand, you could look at this and say, 'Wow, this is really big and intimidating,' but it's not really how I look at it," David explained. "The investigators at the special counsel's office are real people. We're all operating under this framework of laws. And, here's a little secret about the legal business: None of this is rocket science."

Gray continued: "The Mueller prosecutors want to know what information Corsi has. He, by law, has to testify truthfully. There are no ifs, ands, or buts about that. So, we can make a mountain out of a mole hill and get a high-powered D.C. lawyer to turn this into something it's not, or we can do what the law says we have to do a deal with it. And that's what we're going to doing."

David was right. I knew that I had not committed any crimes, not working with Roger Stone, not reporting on the 2016 presidential campaign—not then or ever. If the Department of Justice wanted to indict me for a criminal call, the FBI could have come to the door to arrest me.

Instead of being handed a subpoena, I could have been put in handcuffs at the front door and taken to a federal jail to await a federal criminal arraignment—an appearance before a federal magistrate at which the criminal charges would be placed at court and I would have been asked to plead "guilty" or "not guilty."

My calculation was that David Gray was one of the best lawyers I had ever met, and it did not concern me that he lacked experience in Washington, D.C. In the final analysis, every one of us—including Mueller's prosecutors—are human beings, some brighter than others, but nobody infallible. I was confident David would give my case his full attention. Even though I was not going to be the only case David was representing at the time, I knew David—like me—would be thinking about the case even when he was sleeping. I couldn't ask for more from anyone.

In the final analysis, I also calculated David Gray—a local lawyer from New Jersey—would disarm Mueller's prosecutor. Rather than choosing to hire a high-profile Washington lawyer who would seek to intimidate the feds, I hired a mom-and-pop lawyer who was out to do the right thing—the right thing before the law and their right thing for me, his client. What more evidence would Mueller's prosecutors need before we even got started to know that my goal was to make it easy for them to get everything in the determination to tell them the truth?

Going into what I suspected could reduce to hand-to-hand combat with the federal prosecutors despite my willingness to cooperate, I felt David Gray stood the best chance of being able to talk to the prosecutors—to intervene between the federal prosecutors and me, to better negotiate what was certain to be difficult moments ahead. David's easy and unassuming manner made it easy for him to interact both with clients and with attorneys on the other side of the case.

During my first career in academics, I taught and wrote a college textbook on judicial politics. From that experience, I knew much of practicing law successfully demanded the good negotiating skills I felt David had naturally and from years of legal practice. A high-priced, big-name attorney representing me might both antagonize the prosecutors and lack the understanding or the skills to make the prosecutors see that he was really on their side too, working to assist me tell the truth.

In reality, it would have been foolish to proceed any other way. Lying to Mueller's prosecutors would not work—that was the whole point of the "perjury trap" tactic. The truth is, the only reason to hire a high-profile Washington lawyer is if a person knows they are guilty, and they want to cut the best deal possible. If you're not guilty, hiring a high-profile Washington lawyer was certain to send the wrong message to Mueller's prosecutors, a tactic which could only prolong and make the investigation involving me more difficult.

After our conference at my home, David Gray telephoned Aaron Zelinsky and indicated both that we would be in Washington, D.C. to comply with the subpoena. David also explained to Zelinsky our willingness to cooperate and my desire to turn over my electronic devices.

Zelinsky accepted the proffer graciously, offering to allow David and me to meet privately with the Special Counsel's office in Washington on Thursday, September 6, 2018, the day before I was scheduled to appear before the grand jury. David agreed, formally implementing the strategy we had decided to pursue.

One more issue remained to be discussed.

Through my network of contacts nationally and internationally, I had been advised that Jay Sekulow, President Trump's attorney who I knew through his work as Chief Counselor for the American Center for Law and Justice (ACLJ), was ready to take David Gray's call.

During their phone conversation, Sekulow offered to Gray that the White House was willing to enter into what is known as a mutual defense agreement with us. Under that agreement, we and the White House would be permitted to share information privately about the Special Prosecutor's investigation, with the goal of the White House and me assisting one another in defending ourselves.

At first, David was concerned that entering into a mutual defense agreement with the White House might upset the Special Counselor's office, sending a signal that could seem to contradict our offer to cooperate. After a few days to consider the ramifications of this decision, David telephoned Sekulow to accept the mutual defense offer. After debating the pros and cons, we had decided that anytime we could get the attorney for the President of the United States to offer assistance to us, we needed to be thankful and accept.

Sekulow suggested to David Gray that there was no need to put the mutual defense agreement in writing, explaining that the White House would comply with the verbal agreement. This saved creating a document that might appear later in some relevant legal proceeding or newspaper article.

Heading to Washington to meet Zelinsky and his associates, we felt as prepared as we could be, entering into a situation where the federal prosecutors knew more than we did and held all the cards.

CHAPTER 3

Meet Roger Stone

THE FIRST TIME I spoke with Roger Stone was on February 22, 2016, when I interviewed him by telephone as a follow-up to an article that I had just published in World Net Daily a few days earlier. That article was a review of a book Stone had just co-authored with Saint John Hunt, son of the Watergate burglar E. Howard Hunt, entitled *Jeb! And the Bush Crime Family: The Inside Story of an American Dynasty.*[4]

At that time, Jeb Bush was making a bid during the GOP presidential primaries to follow his father and his brother to the presidency. Stone and Hunt's book was aimed at derailing Jeb Bush's presidential campaign by making sure voters were aware of the dark side of Bush family politics, dating back to Prescott Bush, the father of George H. W. Bush, financing Hitler in the 1930s in conjunction with Brown Brothers Harriman on Wall Street and the Dulles brothers, John Foster Dulles who was secretary of state under President Eisenhower, and Allen Dulles, who headed the CIA under both Presidents Eisenhower and Kennedy.

I recorded this conversation with Stone for my private notes, wanting to make sure I quoted Stone precisely. Although I had followed Stone's career for years, this was the first time we actually spoke with one another. In August 2015, Stone parted as an advisor for Donald Trump's presidential campaign, ensuing a brief controversy

---

4   Stone, Roger; Hunt, Saint John. *Jeb! And the Bush Crime Family: The Inside Story of an American Dynasty* (New York: Skyhorse Publishing, 2016).

over whether Stone resigned, as Stone maintained, or was fired, as Trump maintained.[5]

The outcome was that Stone repositioned himself as an outside adviser. The strategy was typical Roger Stone brilliance. Rather than Trump being branded for the various maneuvers Stone would pull during the campaign to command media attention, Trump could always distance himself from Stone. Known for being a flamboyant showman as well as a shrewd GOP political strategist, Stone was a long-time Trump political adviser who sported a "bad-boy" reputation in politics since his early days as an advisor to Richard Nixon, a relationship that grew after Nixon resigned.

In one of our telephone conversations in February 2016, Stone told me he was still speaking by phone with Trump every day. "Trump doesn't listen to everything I say," Stone admitted candidly. "But I'd say my hit rate is about seven out of ten. But I'm really careful to pick my shots. I try to keep it to structural issues and important stuff, not trying him to get his picture taken with somebody's mother-in-law."

Stone first emerged in GOP politics as a Nixon era "Young Republican," who began his career as contemporaries of both Paul Manafort and Lee Atwater.

Manafort was Stone's choice to replace Corey Lewandowsky as Trump's campaign manager. Manafort was Stone's choice because of Manafort's prior experience herding delegates won in the primary process to make sure they voted for Trump in the first ballot taken at the upcoming GOP National Convention, scheduled for Cleveland that July. A key strategy of Trump's GOP presidential rivals was to deny Trump from getting the required number of delegates to secure the presidential nomination on the first ballot, confident that the

---

5   Caputo, Marc. "Sources: Roger Stone quit, wasn't fired by Trump in campaign shakeup," Politico, August, 8, 2015. *https://www.politico.com/story/2015/08/sources-roger-stone-quit-wasnt-fired-by-donald-trump-in-campaign-shakeup-121177.*

GOP establishment was in sufficient control of the convention rules that Trump could be defeated in the second ballot.

Atwater had a meteoric rise in GOP politics, brandishing aggressive campaign tactics in Ronald Reagan's 1984 re-election campaign and again in George H. W. Bush's 1988 presidential run. Before he died an untimely early death in 1991, Atwater had advanced the "Southern Strategy" first introduced in Nixon's successful 1968 presidential campaign, in an effort to draw working class voters from their traditional allegiance to the Democrats to vote Republican.

Roger Stone combines Atwater's flair for outrageous but effective political strategies with Manafort's quiet competence herding delegates. I quickly realized in talking with Stone that he had managed to brilliantly combine Manafort and Atwater's brilliance. I suspected Stone was more than capable of designing successful strategies to defeat Hillary Clinton's leftist politics, and that the increasingly bare knuckles environment that increasingly typifies American presidential politics would play to Stone's advantage.

"I think only women can defeat Hillary Clinton," Stone argued, outlining his tactics to propel Donald Trump into the White House. "When we criticize Hillary, we are crusty old white guys that allow Hillary to play the victim. See, she will claim we don't like Hillary because we're misogynists, we're sexists, that we resent Hillary because she's a woman. I want the victims of Bill and Hillary's sexual assaults to lead the charge." This explained the 2015 book Stone had co-authored with Robert Morrow, entitled *The Clintons' War on Women*.[6]

"I want women like Kathleen Willey, Paula Jones, Juanita Brodderick, and dozens of others to tell in graphic detail what it's like to be assaulted, overpowered, bitten, groped, and in some cases raped by Bill Clinton. Then I want them to tell how Hillary bullied them, threatened them, terrorized them into silence," he continued. "Then

---

6   Stone, Roger and Morrow, Robert. *The Clintons' War on Women* (New York: Skyhorse Publishing, 2015).

let women decide. Let millennial women who may be thinking about voting for Hillary Clinton without knowing very much about her know the truth and decide for themselves."

Stone explained this was one of two key strategies he had developed to chip away marginal voters from the voting blocs Hillary would need to win the general election.

"The other is this laughable notion that African-Americans will vote for her," Stone continued. "Bill Clinton has an abandoned, rejected African-American son. Danny Williams is Bill Clinton's son, but he was banished not because Bill rejected him, but because Hillary would have none of it. I have an Arkansas State Trooper who told me that he brought Christmas presents to the small shack where Danny Williams lived with his drug-addicted mother.

Stone continued: "She was the black prostitute Bill was with on thirteen definite occasions, and Bill is definitely Danny's father. But Hillary is the one who banished Danny. So, Hillary can say, 'Black Lives Matter,' but apparently, they don't matter if you are Danny Williams. You are going to be seeing Danny Williams on TV a lot this coming fall."

As Trump won the GOP presidential nomination on the first ballot and the race entered the final phase with Trump facing off against Hillary for the presidency, I came to appreciate just how much Stone's strategic thinking influenced the shape and direction of the Trump campaign.

Granted, Trump had many issues on which to run, as witnessed by the "Lock Her Up," "Build That Wall," and "Drain the Swamp" chants crowds at every Trump campaign rally in the final months reveled in shouting out. Still the issues of Hillary and Bill Clinton's tag-team sexual aggression and Danny Williams continued to dog Hillary's campaign, chipping away at the margins of her women and African-American voters. A fundamental principle of the modern political campaign is that successful candidates must cut into the percentages their opponents expect to get from key voting blocs loyal to the opponent's political party.

Another reality of modern politics is the mainstream media has become a Deep State lapdog, willingly reporting the policy preferences and opinions of the Democratic Party in a way that previous generations would have recognized as propaganda—biased opinion-based ideological interpretations of politics presented by the mainstream media as objective truth.

My relationship with Stone began developing into a friendship and a working partnership, starting with a dinner in February 2016 at the Harvard Club in New York City. On this, our first meeting, I found Stone presented himself in person with the sartorial flair for which he was well-known. Wearing a handsome, British bespoke made-to-order suit with a matching tie and pocket handkerchief and a spread collar tailored white dress shirt, Stone looked every bit the fashion statement that he in truth was. With his platinum white hair neatly combed back, Stone broadcast an appearance that matched his reputation that in matters of political warfare, Stone was both brilliant and, when necessary, devious.

We began with martinis, proceeded to a vintage French Bordeaux, topped off by the Harvard Club's London-style roast beef special. By the time the dinner was over, it was clear our complementary skills in politics could be combined to Donald Trump's benefit. I bought into Stone's strategy for chipping away to draw voters from the margins of Hillary's voter base among women and African-Americans. I resolved to work with Stone to develop a close working relationship with the WND editors and staff writers, starting with myself.

As I mentioned earlier, Joseph Farah had maintained a policy where staff news reporters, including me, were also encouraged to write commentaries typically known as "op-ed," an abbreviation for "opinion editorial." In this spirit, the WND managing editors encouraged me to develop a close relationship with Stone. Throughout the 2016 campaign, I conferred with Stone by telephone frequently, designing with him WND coverage of various publicity moves Stone undertook to drive the national news cycle to cover Donald Trump more favorably. Truthfully, the "resist and obstruct" movement against Trump had already evidenced itself during the campaign, as mainstream media editors and reporters sought to turn Trump's words and policies into controversies damaging to Trump. My goal was to use the internet to counter the mainstream bias by advancing Trump's cause with WND's large Judeo-Christian conservative readership.

As happens all too often in politics, unexpected events often shape the nature and outcome of political races. This was abundantly clear in the 2016 presidential election. The key outside event in 2016 involved WikiLeaks and the drop of previously confidential information that proved extremely damaging to the Democratic National Committee and to Hillary Clinton's presidential campaign.

The first WikiLeaks drop occurred on March 16, 2016, with WikiLeaks releasing a searchable archive of 30,000 emails and email attachments, comprising 50,547 pages of documents that spanned the time period from June 30, 2010 through August 12, 2014. In releasing the emails, WikiLeaks noted the emails had been made available in the form of thousands of PDF files that the State Department provided as a result of a Freedom of Information Act (FOIA) request.[7]

This WikiLeaks release did not cause the same stir as 2010 when WikiLeaks began to release serially a trove of classified diplomatic cables dating back to the 1960s but continuing through Hillary Clinton's years as secretary of state that had been stolen by Chelsea Manning, previously known as U.S. Army Private Bradley Manning. The documents in the WikiLeaks search had been public since the State Department began releasing Clinton emails since May 2015,

---

7   "Hillary Clinton Email Archive," WikiLeaks.org, March 16, 2016. *https://wikileaks.org/clinton-emails/*.

when it was first disclosed that Secretary of State Clinton had used a private email server to conduct official State Department business.[8]

The real WikiLeaks earthquake occurred on Friday, July 22, 2016, when WikiLeaks began releasing over two days 44,053 emails and 17,761 attachments that included Democratic National Committee emails from top DNC officials.[9] Julian Assange timed the release of the DNC emails to be the Friday before the DNC National Nominating Convention was scheduled to open that Monday, July 25, 2016, in Philadelphia, Pennsylvania. The particularly damaging aspect of this two-day email release was that many of the records revealed details from within the DNC documenting that Rep. Debbie Wasserman Schultz, Florida, who then chaired the DNC, had plotted with the Clinton campaign to rig the primaries so as to assure that Bernie Sanders would not get the Democratic Party presidential nomination.

By Sunday, July 24, 2016, Wasserman Schultz announced her intention to resign as chair of the DNC, as a direct result of the controversy over the Sanders campaign fueled by the DNC emails released by WikiLeaks. The DNC announced that Donna Brazile, a long-time Clinton loyalist, would step up from vice chair of the DNC to serve as interim DNC chair until such time as a permanent replacement could be selected.[10] As it became apparent the thousands of DNC emails published by WikiLeaks had been stolen from DNC computer servers, Robby Mook, Clinton's campaign manager, told ABC's "This Week" on Sunday, July 24, 2016, that the emails had been hacked

---

8   Blake, Andrew. "Hillary Clinton's email archive made searchable by WikiLeaks," March 17, 2016.

9   "Search the DNC email database," WikiLeaks.org, July 22, 2016. *https://wikileaks.org/dnc-emails/*.

10   Martin, Jonathan and Rappeport, Alan. "Debbie Wasserman Schultz to Resign D.N.C. Post," *New York Times*, July 24, 2016. *https://www.nytimes.com/2016/07/25/us/politics/debbie-wasserman-schultz-dnc-wikileaks-emails.html*.

by the Russians and leaked to WikiLeaks "for the purpose of helping Donald Trump."[11]

The WikiLeaks release of DNC emails on the eve of the DNC convention beginning in Philadelphia was catastrophic to Hillary Clinton's campaign. The information exchanged in the emails among and between top DNC officials validated Bernie Sanders' complaint that Wasserman Schultz in a conspiracy with the Clinton campaign had stolen the nomination, largely a smear campaign that attacked Sanders on religious grounds by spreading the rumor Sanders was an atheist. Moreover, the emails showed evidence the DNC manipulation of the primaries focused on "Super Delegates" who went for Hillary, with the result Clinton got almost as many delegates as did Sanders in several primary contests that were critical to winning the nomination.

Instead of throwing a nationally televised party with a united Democratic Party nominating Clinton for president, the WikiLeaks release of DNC emails threw the convention into chaos, with Sanders stoking the anger of his supporters. "There's no question in my mind and I think there's no question in any objective observer's mind that the DNC was supporting Hillary Clinton and was in opposition to our campaign, so I'm not shocked by this and that is why many, many times I made clear Debbie Wasserman Schultz should resign," Sanders said on the nationally televised talk shows the Sunday before the gavel went down to open the DNC on Monday.[12]

On Monday, July 25, 2016, WikiLeaks founder Julian Assange in a Skype interview with Richard Engel for "NBC Nightly News"

---

11   Sanger, David E. and Perlroth, Nicole. "As Democrats Gather, a Russian Subplot Raises Intrigue," *New York Times*, July 24, 2016. *https://www.nytimes.com/2016/07/25/us/politics/donald-trump-russia-emails.html?module=inline*.

12   "Bernie calls for party chairwoman's head as she's dropped from convention over leaked emails revealing plans to 'smear' Sanders," Mail Online, July 24, 2016.

argued that "there is no proof whatsoever" that his organization got the hacked DNC emails from Russia. Assange further asserted WikiLeaks was planning to release another round of emails that would provide "enough evidence" to indict Hillary Clinton.[13] This was a clear tipoff from Assange that the DNC emails published on the eve of the DNC convention were not all the DNC stolen emails that WikiLeaks had and planned to publish. From this point on, reporters and political pundits speculated about just what more Assange had on the DNC and when he might drop the bomb.

Then, on August 21, 2016, Roger Stone infamously tweeted the following: "Trust me, it will soon be the Podesta's time in the barrel." On October 7, 2016, WikiLeaks began publishing in a serial drip-by-drip fashion, what came to a total of 57,153 emails that WikiLeaks termed "The Podesta File," after John Podesta, the chair of Hillary Clinton's 2016 presidential campaign. The final WikiLeaks post was numbered "Post 34," dropped by WikiLeaks on November 7, 2016, three days after the presidential election was held.

This coincidence raised speculation that Podesta had advanced knowledge tracing back to August 2016, permitting him to know the final cache of DNC emails in WikiLeaks' possession involved John Podesta—something Assange never suggested publicly in advance of the first email drop in the "Podesta File" that occurred on October 7, 2016. If the July 2017 drop of DNC emails implicating Wasserman Schultz in the Sanders scandal was devastating to the launch of Hillary's campaign, the never-ending day-by-day publication of the Podesta emails was devastating to the conclusion of Hillary's campaign.

---

13   "WikiLeaks' Julian Assange: 'No Proof' Hacked DNC Emails
      Came from Russia," July 25, 2018. h*ttps://www.nbcnews.com/news/
      us-news/wikileaks-julian-assange-no-proof-hacked-dnc-emails-came-
      russia-n616541*. See also: Sanger, David E. "F.B.I. looks closer at email
      hacking; Agency wants to find out whether those close to Clinton were
      exposed," *International New York Times*, July 27, 2016.

Democratic opponents of Trump raised the question that if Roger Stone had known in advance that Assange was holding the Podesta emails, as evidenced by his tweet on August 21, was it possible Stone had colluded with the Russians and with WikiLeaks? Had all this happened by accident or were the WikiLeaks DNC email drops just Roger Stone's crowning achievement in a career distinguished by dirty tricks. Put simply: Did Roger Stone coordinate with Russia to steal the DNC emails and give them to WikiLeaks, having arranged with Assange in advance a strategy to use the hacked DNC emails to prevent Hillary from achieving the White House?

Other steps taken by Roger Stone during the campaign also suggested Stone was in touch with a mysterious hacker known as "Guccifer 2.0," a hacker U.S. intelligence sources believed was a name used to mask a group of Russian hackers who were responsible for stealing the DNC emails in the first place.

On July 13, 2016, Guccifer 2.0, a hacker who previously claimed to have breached the computers of the DNC, released a cache of purported DNC documents to *The Hill*, a widely respected Washington-based news source. The documents included spreadsheets with more than 11,000 DNC donors, plus various DNC opposition research studies on Donald Trump. "Our experts are confident in their assessment that the Russian government hackers were the actors responsible for the breach detected in April, and we believe that the subsequent release and the claims around it may be a part of a disinformation campaign by the Russians," a senior DNC official said in a written statement published by *The Hill*.[14]

On July 15, 2018, the *New York Times* reported that WikiLeaks had been seeking stolen files from Guccifer 2.0, tracing back to

---

14   Uchill, Joe. "Guccifer 2.0 releases new DNC documents," The Hill, July 13, 2016. *https://thehill.com/policy/cybersecurity/287558-guccifer-20-drops-new-dnc-docs*.

June 2016, when the DNC first revealed the DNC servers had been hacked.[15] The *Times* reported that private messages cited in Mueller's indictment on July 13, 2016, charged twelve Russian intelligence officers of trying to interfere in the 2016 presidential elections. According to the *New York Times*, Mueller was in possession of documents from WikiLeaks communicating to Guccifer 2.0 in 2016 that publishing the DNC information Guccifer 2.0 stole on the WikiLeaks site will "have a much higher impact than what you are doing."

The *New York Times* suggested this exchange between WikiLeaks and Guccifer 2.0 offered "a new look at the central role of Guccifer 2.0, the digital persona alleged to have been set up by Russian military intelligence, which passed the stolen Democratic documents and misinformation to WikiLeaks and some Americans, who then spread it through social media and news organizations."

Roger Stone's contacts with Guccifer 2.0 began in August 2016. Stone wrote on his blog StoneColdTruth.com that his contacts with Guccifer 2.0 began on August 14, 2016, when he noticed on his Twitter feed that Guccifer 2.0, who had been suspended by Twitter, had been reinstated.[16] Stone sent Guccifer 2.0 a direct message on Twitter saying, "Delighted you are reinstated." This led to an exchange that included additional direct messages via Twitter with Guccifer 2.0 on August 17, 2016, that Stone has termed "benign, innocent and even banal exchanges." Guccifer 2.0 made another attempt to have a direct message conversation with Stone via Twitter on September 9,

---

15   Sanger, David E.; Rutenberg, Jim; and Lipton, Eric. "Tracing Guccifer 2.0's Many Tentacles in the 2016 Election," *New York Times*, July 15, 2018. *https://www.nytimes.com/2018/07/15/us/politics/guccifer-russia-mueller.html.*

16   Stone, Roger. "Roger Stone: The Smoking Gun Aims, Fires, Misses," StoneColdTruth.com, March 10, 2017. *https://stonecoldtruth.com/roger-stone-the-smoking-gun-aims-fires-misses/.*

2016, but Stone insists his side of the conversation consisted merely of a request to repost a link, which Guccifer 2.0 agreed to do.[17]

According to the indictment filed by Mueller against the twelve Russian hackers, Guccifer 2.0 was actually operated by a group of Russian military intelligence officers based in Moscow. The indictment further alleges the Russians used Guccifer 2.0 to send multiple messages "to a person who was in regular contact with senior members" of Trump's campaign.[18] Clearly, Stone's tweets with Guccifer 2.0 target him as a likely suspect for that person, especially given that Stone remained in regular contact with Trump even after Stone resigned as Trump's political advisor.

On August 28, 2018, when I was served the subpoena from the Mueller grand jury, I suspected immediately the prosecutors in the Special Counsel office were in possession of evidence that suggested I might have been the link between Stone and Assange. As David Gray and I prepared to go to Washington, we speculated Mueller may have targeted me as the link who provided Stone his advance knowledge in August 2016 that Assange possessed DNC emails from John Podesta that WikiLeaks planned to release serially over a number of days as the 2016 "October Surprise," designed to deal a knock-out punch to the Clinton campaign. If I was Stone's link to Assange, was this the connection with WikiLeaks that Stone used to get WikiLeaks the Guccifer 2.0 hacks of the DNC computers?

---

17   Stone, Roger. "Guccifer 2.0 Not a Russian Hacker," StoneColdTruth.com, October 11, 2017. *https://stonecoldtruth.com/ guccifer-2-0-not-a-russian-hacker/*.

18   Helderman, Rosalind S. and Roig-Franzia, Manuel. "Charges against Russian intelligence officers intensify spotlight on Trump adviser Roger Stone," *New York Times*, July 13, 2018. *https://www. washingtonpost.com/politics/charges-against-russian-intelligence-officers-intensify-spotlight-on-trump-adviser-roger-stone/2018/07/13/ ba0d0caa-86bb-11e8-8553-a3ce89036c78_story.html?utm_term=. f665b4f372df.*

CHAPTER 4

We Head to Washington

ON WEDNESDAY, SEPTEMBER 5, 2018, I took the Amtrak train from Newark Airport to Washington, D.C., to be in place a night prior to our scheduled interview with the Special Counselor's office the next day. While I had prepared the best I could, I really had no idea if I were a criminal target of the Special Prosecutor's investigation, or what the prosecutors would ask.

I had reserved rooms for myself and for David Gray at the Mayflower Hotel on Connecticut Avenue. The Mayflower is a landmark, historic hotel, built in 1925, that has been visited by every president since Calvin Coolidge. The first time I was in the Mayflower Hotel was in the 1950s with my father. The Mayflower was one of his favorite hotels.

Centrally located downtown a few blocks from the White House, everyone in D.C. knows the Mayflower. The Mayflower is much like the Plaza Hotel was in New York City before the Plaza was converted to condominiums. If you told someone from New York that you were in town staying at the Plaza, the Plaza needed no more introduction. Immediately, the New Yorker would recognize you were staying at one of the best hotels in the city, conveying your knowledge of the city as an insider and your obvious success in life being able to afford a luxury hotel.

As a child, I had always been surprised all the staff at the Plaza in New York and the Mayflower in D.C. knew my father by name. Then, one day I saw my father hand the doorman a twenty-dollar bill as a tip. "I don't have to pay that person salary, benefits, or taxes," my father explained to me. "Yet for the price of a twenty-dollar bill, that person would do anything for me."

In the 1960s, my father established a corporate account for the railroad union executives at Paul Young's restaurant, an elegant restaurant located in the basement of a building directly across the street from the Mayflower. Decorated in red and highlighted by heavy chandeliers, a grand staircase descending from the street entrance to the basement dining room permitted a grand entry. Whenever I was in Washington, well into the 1970s, my father insisted I have dinner at the restaurant.

Paul Young's restaurant was a hangout for the Kennedy family when it first opened in 1960. On the evening of Jack Kennedy's inauguration, the Kennedy family hosted a private party for 350 people in Paul Young's restaurant. In the years the restaurant was open, Presidents Johnson, Nixon, Ford, and Carter all dined there. At Paul Young's, I was always presented with a menu with no prices. At the end of the meal, there was no check to pay. The meal went on my father's corporate account.[19]

For years in the late 1980s, I virtually lived in the Plaza in New York City, while I was working for a bank marketing firm headquartered in Portland, Oregon, that at that time was leading the nation in the business of third-party marketing establishing annuity and mutual fund retail sales in savings and loan associations as well as in commercial banks. My father's insight worked well both at the Plaza and at the Mayflower. I chose the Mayflower because from experience, I knew David Gray and I would be able to establish ourselves with the staff, getting the special treatment and privacy protection we would need.

Given prior commitments, David Gray had to drive to Washington from New Jersey on Thursday morning. So, I had Wednesday

---

19   See: DeFerrari, John. Historic Restaurants of Washington, D.C.: Capital Eats (The History Press, 2013).

evening to myself. On the next block south along Connecticut Avenue was Morton's Steakhouse—one of the few restaurants in Washington where you can smoke a cigar. For dinner that evening, I headed to the second-floor patio of Morton's to begin dinner with a cigar and a martini.

Admittedly, I am a creature of habit. Liking the Mayflower, I find it hard to stay anywhere else in Washington. Knowing Morton's is across the street, I'm happy to head there for a steady dinner every night that I am in town. Rather than being bored by the repetition, I follow my father's advice that by tipping well I would be certain to become a "regular" customer known and taken care of at both places.

On Thursday, September 6, 2018, I kept in touch with David Gray by cellphone, monitoring his progress along Interstate 95 as he headed south from New Jersey. David arrived at the Mayflower about a half-hour before the FBI was scheduled to pick us up at the Mayflower to transport us to the FBI building in southeast D.C. for the interview.

At approximately 1:30 p.m., FBI Agent Smith called David Gray's cellphone letting him know the FBI car was in front of the Mayflower Hotel as scheduled. Since we were visiting the Special Prosecutor voluntarily, the FBI extended this courtesy of transporting us to and from the FBI building.

As I pushed the button for the elevator to go down to the Mayflower's lobby, I turned to David and said, "David, you are about to walk into history." While the thought must have occurred to David previously, I knew it was not possible for anyone to anticipate the ferocity of the Washington maelstrom until you had experienced the storm directly.

I had been on a national stage several times before, but for David, a small business and family attorney from New Jersey, this was certain to be a life-changing experience. Little did I know at that moment, the truth was this was about to be a life-changing experience for both of us.

Exiting the Mayflower, David and I were greeted by Agent Smith and a second agent whom we will call Agent Roberts. The FBI on formal missions typically work in teams of two, both for security and for having a better chance of remembering accurately everything that was said. Getting into Agent Smith's FBI-issue SUV, I assumed David and I were under surveillance and that everything we said would be reported by these two FBI agents.

Having had extensive experience in my career working with the FBI in a professional capacity, I realized that FBI agents typically are well-trained, highly intelligent federal law enforcement employees with private lives that have much in common with the average middle class American. Since we had about forty minutes in D.C. increasingly impossible downtown traffic to get to the FBI building where the interview was scheduled, I decided we needed to make the ride comfortable. I began, as I typically begin conversations meeting someone new, by asking Agents Smith and Roberts to tell me about themselves.

Agent Smith shared that he had just spent a number of years working for the FBI in Albuquerque, New Mexico. This proved of interest to me since I lived in New Mexico from 1976 through 1979 when I had worked as a research professor at the University of New Mexico. In those years, I had conducted for the National Science Foundation one of the largest random-assignment field studies ever conducted to test a public policy issue. On behalf of the New Mexico Department of scientific Employment, we started by testing whether due process could be delivered if *Goldberg v. Kelly* "fair hearings" if unemployment cases were conducted by telephone.

Ultimately, I finished the "Fair Hearing Project" at the University of Denver, after the New Mexico Department of Human Services had joined the field test to see if welfare fair hearings could be held by telephone. After four years and over $1 million dollars in federal funding from the National Science Foundation, the U.S. Labor Department, the U.S. Health and Human Services Department, and the U.S. Immigration and Naturalization Service, the research proved telephone fair hearings were equivalent to in-person hearings in delivering due process. This resulted in a nationwide policy change allowing government agencies to conduct *Goldberg v. Kelly*-type hearings by telephone, saving hundreds of millions of dollars in unnecessary travel.

On the remainder of the ride to the FBI building in southeast D.C., we exchanged stories about New Mexico living, including a love for New Mexico's brand of southwest cuisine that Agent Smith and I share.

Arriving at the FBI building, we noticed it appeared to be an ordinary office building, carrying no obvious identification as an FBI building. From the street, Agent Smith entered the building into a loading dock where another FBI agent was inside, waiting for his cellphone call to open the door to the street. Agent Smith commented that the FBI was doing this as a courtesy to us, given that we had proffered to provide evidence voluntarily, and that the tinted windows of his SUV would prevent the news photographers on the street from identifying us for press reports. Once the public door of the loading dock was closed, we exited the vehicle.

Inside, Agents Smith and Roberts, along with the FBI agent at the dock, entered the building through the basement, finding ourselves in a secure room with lockers. Here we were asked to lock up securely our cellphones and all electronic equipment, including our laptops. David held possession of the keys to the lock compartments, making it clear we had not handed these devices over to the FBI, but were complying with the restriction not to bring any electronic devices inside the building. Agent Smith took possession of my MacBook Pro laptop, my MacBook Air, the external storage device for the Time Machine, and my cellphone, since we planned to hand these over to the Special Prosecutor at the upcoming interview.

Agent Smith accompanied us to an inside conference room large enough to dwarf the large conference table and chairs arranged to accommodate as many as some twenty persons. The two walls of the conference room to my right and my left had chalk boards. A few scattered chairs scantly filled the empty space. There were no windows. David and I were instructed to sit on one side of the table. Agent Smith noted we were not permitted to leave the room unaccompanied, noting that an FBI agent would accompany us to the bathroom door as needed. David and I were left alone for a few minutes waiting for the meeting to start.

At about 2:30 p.m., Aaron Zelinsky entered the room, introduced himself, shook hands with us, and took a chair directly across from me on the other side of the conference table. In the few minutes we had before the meeting started, I did my customary introductory ritual of asking Zelinsky to tell me about himself. "Where were you born?" I asked. Zelinsky explained that he was of Polish descent and that he was the grandson of two Jewish Poles who had survived the Auschwitz concentration camp during World War II. "My grandmother was on the death march the Nazis led out of Auschwitz as the war was coming to a close," he noted. "She was liberated in Germany, outside Heidelberg, having walked there from Poland.

I shared with Zelinsky that I had visited Auschwitz and Birkenau twice when I was consulting in the 1990s with Polish banks after the end of communism in Poland in 1989. Both times I was at Auschwitz were in the depths of winter. I recall wearing a heavy wool overcoat and boots. "I know from those visits the horror of a Polish winter," I said. "I can't imagine her courage at surviving." I asked how she managed to get to the United States since many concentration camp survivors were liberated by the Russian Army, with all too many surviving the concentration camp only to die in a Soviet Russian Gulag. Zelinsky explained that his grandmother managed to get herself into the American sector before she surrendered to the military police.[20]

---

20   Peak, Christopher. "New Haven natives take key roles in Russian probe," *New Haven Independent*, June 25, 2017. *https://ctmirror. org/2017/06/25/new-haven-natives-take-key-roles-in-russia-probe/.*

I subsequently learned that on his desk, Zelinsky has often kept an old photograph of his grandfather Jacob Dronski, a Pole who covertly helped the Americans during World War II, beside a framed letter from June 17, 1946. The letter was from a U.S. Army captain stationed in Bavaria, Germany, praising Zelinsky's grandfather for his service to U.S. military special investigators pursuing Nazis after the war, for which he recommended Zelinsky's grandfather for American citizenship. I shared with Zelinsky how deeply affected I have been by the visits I have paid to Yad Vashem, the Holocaust museum in Jerusalem. I commented that over the years an increasing part of Yad Vashem has been devoted to memorializing the Jewish resistance to the Nazis during the war.

Zelinsky also commented that his wife had graduated from Gilmour Academy, a Catholic college-preparatory day and boarding school located in the Gates Mills suburb of Cleveland, Ohio. Zelinsky knew I had graduated from St. Ignatius High School on Cleveland's West Side in the 1960s. In that era, my girlfriends tended to come from Magnificat, a Catholic girl's school in Rocky River, Ohio. But at the Ignatius mixers I remember attending as a high school student, the girls from Gilmour were always in attendance.

Next to enter the conference room were prosecutors Jeannie Rhee and Andrew Goldstein. Jeannie Rhee, born in 1972, had served in the Office of Legal Counsel at the Department of Justice and as an assistant U.S. attorney for the District of Columbia. In 2011, Rhee joined the Washington D.C. office of law firm WilmerHale, where she served as a partner in the Litigation Division, advising clients who were the subject of government investigations, including white-collar criminal investigations.[21] Like Zelinsky, Rhee also got her BA degree

---

21   "Former DOJ Counsel Jeanine Rhee Rejoins WilmerHale," February 24, 2011. WilmerHale.com, *https://www.wilmerhale.com/en/insights/news/ former-doj-counsel-jeannie-rhee-rejoins-wilmerhale-february-24-2011.*

from Yale, where she graduated summa cum laude, and her JD from the Yale Law School.

Andrew Goldstein graduated from Princeton University in 1996 and received his law degree from Yale. In 2010, he joined the U.S. Attorney's Office for the Southern District of New York, where he became the chief of the public corruption unit under U.S. Attorney Prett Baharara. Working as a reporter, I had covered several cases where Goldstein was involved. I knew him as an experienced criminal investigator who had seen come and go every type of crook and swindler the worst in New York City can produce. Goldstein was known to be an expert in money laundering cases. Goldstein was reportedly heading for Mueller with the separate investigation into the business and real estate dealings of former Trump campaign manager Paul Manafort.[22]

Like Rhee, Mueller also worked for Washington-based "white-shoe law firm" WilmerHale, where he left a reported 3.4 million-dollar job representing clients such as Facebook, Apple, Sony, and the NFL.[23]

So, here I was, a Harvard Ph.D. in Political Science, facing three experienced prosecutors trained at Yale Law School. In 1968, when I was accepted at Harvard Graduate School, I was also accepted at Harvard Law School. The Political Science Department at Harvard offered me a National Science Foundation fellowship which paid all my tuition and fees, plus a living stipend of $1,000 a month, big

22   "These are the lawyers on Robert Mueller's special counsel team," CBS News, last updated September 20, 2017. *https://www.cbsnews.com/news/these-are-the-lawyers-on-robert-muellers-special-counsel-team/.*

23   Zapotosky, Matt. "Mueller, several team members gave up million-dollar jobs to work on special counsel investigation," *Washington Post*, August 8, 2017. *https://www.washingtonpost.com/world/national-security/mueller-several-team-members-gave-up-million-dollar-jobs-to-work-on-special-counsel-investigation/2017/08/08/e11169da-7b78-11e7-83c7-5bd5460f0d7e_story.html?utm_term=.3a7cfd0a6762.*

money for a graduate student at that time. In contrast, the Law School offered no scholarship. In 1968, Harvard did not have a joint Ph.D./JD program. Here I was decades later, wishing I took a few years longer and gotten my law degree at Harvard after I got a Ph.D., regardless what it might have cost.

At the FBI conference table, Rhee sat on Zelinsky's right, directly across from David Gray. Goldstein sat at the end of the table, out of my eyesight when I was addressing Zelinsky or Rhee—a perfect position from which to observe every detail without me being able to easily watch him. The rest of the FBI's table was filled by six FBI agents, plus Heather Agostino, a DOJ analyst. Zelinsky was leading the investigation into my case. Rhee was clearly acting as Zelinsky's senior, obviously in charge of overseeing this investigation. With the exception of a question or two asked by Heather Agostino, Rhee and Zelinsky were virtually the only two on the government's side who spoke once the formal interview began.

We started with Zelinsky noting that I was appearing voluntarily under a proffer advanced by my attorney David Gray. Zelinsky recited what amounted to my rights, reminding me that lying to the FBI was a federal criminal felony. He added intentional "forgetting" was also a federal criminal felony if the memory failure was due to a witness ploy to mislead or misdirect the FBI. I acknowledged that I understood and that to the best of my ability, I intended to be truthful, as evidenced by our handing over to the FBI these various electronic devices.

Zelinsky commented upon an obvious closed-circuit camera cover mounted on the ceiling at the wall to our left. "We are not recording this meeting," he said, "and we presume you are not recording the meeting either." David Gray acknowledged that we were not recording the meeting. Even though the meeting was not being recorded, I suspected there could be FBI agents in a separate room analyzing the dynamics of the meeting. Very possibly, some of the FBI agents at the table were experts in the use of behavioral and verbal clues to detect lying. While the meeting was not being recorded, at least one of the FBI agents was taking detailed notes of the meeting, as was David Gray.

When it was our turn, David Gray began the process of handing over my two computers, my external backup device, and my cellphone. This process took some time, as an FBI agent filled out the necessary consent form for me to sign and carefully took down all the usernames and passwords required to access the devices.

Once this was complete, Jeanie Rhee took over, making it a point to tell David and me how much the Special Counsel appreciated our willingness to cooperate with their investigation. Handing these devices over voluntarily saved the FBI the time and expense of obtaining a search warrant to obtain them. I pointed out the FBI now should be able to recover most if not all of my emails from 2016, even if I subsequently erased them, given that the time machine since I purchased the seventeen-inch MacBook Pro laptop backed up the computer with a permanent record four times a month.

The interview was off to a positive note, though I remained nervous sitting across from this army of federal law enforcement agents conscious that anything I said that could be construed to be a lie could send me to federal prison.

For the first hour or so, the FBI questioned details of my biography and my association with Donald Trump and Roger Stone. I noted that I first met Donald Trump when I stayed as a regular guest, "just about living at the Plaza Hotel," in the years when Trump owned the hotel. While I did not recount my father's advice to the Special Counsel, I recalled that the policy of handing out twenty dollar tips was sufficient in the 1990s for the Plaza Hotel staff at the front door one day to move President Trump's limo from in front of the Plaza to make room for the stretch limo I had when I was doing the bank marketing operating from New York City, starting in the mid-1980s. I knew Trump well in that era and my family and I were regularly invited to Trump's private New Year's Parties in the Plaza through the 1990s.

I also noted that Trump placed a series of phone calls to me in 2011 to ask about Barack Obama's birth certificate, as I was about to publish my book *Where's the Birth Certificate* in March 2011. During the 2016 presidential campaign, I received press credentials from the Trump campaign and I attended in person the press conference in the lobby of the Trump Plaza when Trump signed the GOP "loyalty pledge" on September 3, 2015, agreeing to support the GOP presidential candidate, even if that candidate were someone other than Donald Trump.

During the campaign, I only recall seeing Trump once up close, and that was as Trump was entering the elevator at Trump Tower. On that occasion, Trump jokingly pointed at me and said, "That's trouble there." The last time I recall having a telephone conversation with Trump was in 2011.

I also recounted for the Special Counsel that sometime in September 2016, I met with Michael Cohen in his office. Cohen introduced me to Corey Lewandowsky, at that time Trump's campaign manager, and to Hope Hicks, Trump's media spokesperson. This is when I first asked for press credentials for WND.com from the campaign and I was surprised that Lewandowsky and Hicks were the only two occupying the entire floor of Trump Towers that later became campaign headquarters.

After a couple of hours, Zelinsky suggested we take a break. When we resumed, the interview changed directions. Zelinsky, seemingly relaxed from the initial discussion, surprisingly said to me when we resumed, "Why don't you drive this interview for a while." This caught me by surprise. Typically, an interview with law enforcement is led by the law enforcement officers in charge. Your goal, as the person being interviewed, is to answer questions, not to direct the meeting.

Immediately, I went to a conclusory statement, seeking to shortcut the process.

"I have never met with Julian Assange and I have never spoken with Julian Assange," I asserted, suspecting the issue of my connection with Assange was at the heart of their interview. From the moment I got the subpoena, I suspected Mueller was investigating whether I was the link that connected Roger Stone, and hence the Trump campaign, to Assange.

Zelinsky asked if Stone wanted to talk to Assange and whether Stone wanted me to get in touch with Assange.

I explained to Zelinsky that in 1981, I had written an academic paper titled "Terrorism as a Desperate Game" that was published in the Journal of Conflict Resolution published at Yale University, a leading game theory journal at the time. The article published a mathematical model I had developed that allowed a computer to predict the outcomes of terrorist events. I received requests for reprints from intelligence agencies around the world.

As result of this publication, I was invited to give a speech at the National Academy of Science in Washington. Subsequently, I was contacted by the State Department through the Agency for International Development. Ultimately, I was given a Top-Secret clearance to join a team of international psychiatrists who were developing hostage-survival techniques and training for State Department personnel in dangerous assignments around the world.

"As I result of that experience, I told Stone, 'No,' that I would not contact Assange or ask anyone to get in touch with Assange," I explained. "I knew that from the moment I contacted Julian Assange, I would be under investigation from several different intelligence agencies, including those of the U.S. government." Besides, I asserted to Mueller's team, even if Assange had told me what Democratic National Committee emails he had and what he planned to do with them, no one would believe me. I argued that I had decided to wait until Assange published the emails. Then, I could write about the stolen emails without being involved in an investigation.

After a few more questions, the meeting blew up. Zelinsky asked for a break as he, Rhee, Goldstein, and the FBI agents all walked out of the meeting. After a few minutes, Goldstein reappeared and asked David Gray to meet with them. My immediate suspicion was that the FBI had information that would contradict my denial. At approximately 4:30 p.m. EST, I sat in the room alone as David and the Special Counsel's team had a discussion in another room.

I could occasionally hear some loud talking coming from the other room, and later into the conversation, what sounded like laughter. Left alone, I got to imagine that I could experience the rest of my life as a felon, with no choice but to spend some time in a federal penitentiary. Worst of all, I was sure that what I had said about Assange was the truth. I did not want to see Assange and I never made an effort to meet him, precisely because I did not want to be under intelligence agency investigation.

This was an extremely tense and stressful hour-and-a-half that I was left alone wondering what was going on in the other room. I concluded that it was in my favor that the conversation was continuing this long. It does not take long to say "no," or to end the meeting with a conclusion that I would be indicted for lying to the FBI. I also felt that through the camera device on the wall at the ceiling to my right was an observation device.

I suspected Zelinsky had been planning to spring a perjury trap on me simply to increase the psychological pressure of the moment. Rather than pace around the room, I decided to sit patiently at the conference table and wait. To pass the time, I found myself replaying mentally Beethoven's Fifth Piano Concerto in E Flat, one of my favorite compositions from the moment I first heard it, when I was a graduate student at Harvard.

Finally, David came back into the room. "We're done for today," he said to me quietly. "They want you as a witness. The grand jury is called off for tomorrow and we are going to return to continue this interview next week."

David finished his explanation when Rhee and Zelinsky re-entered the room. Both were visibly agitated.

"We have demonstrable proof that what you said was false," Zelinsky announced. Rhee added that she was pleased I did not give the answer about Assange before the grand jury. "It would be extremely difficult to expunge that testimony from the record," she said. Both made it clear that I was not a target to the investigation, but that I had to be truthful. Zelinsky repeated what David had told me. "We are going to give you a week to examine your 2016 emails and come back," he said. "We are done here for today."

Left alone, David and I packed up our papers. The FBI escorted us out of the building, back through the secure room where David had left his cellphone and other electronic devices. In the loading dock, we got back into Agent Smith's SUV and were driven politely and efficiently back to the Mayflower Hotel.

Packing up to go, I realized the problem was that I had not been able to review my 2016 emails before meeting with the FBI.

The problem was in large part a technical problem. I had turned over my MacBook Pro laptop to the FBI in the condition it was in the last day I used it, sometime in 2017. This prevented me from reloading from the Time Machine my 2016 emails before the interview with the Special Counsel. Reloading the 2016 emails would have erased all the information currently on the laptop and I did not want the FBI thinking I had reloaded the 2016 emails because I wanted to destroy evidence. The way the Time Machine worked, I could not read earlier time emails unless I completely restored the computer to a given date as recorded in the Time Machine. That would wipe out the current state of the computer on the day of the reload.

Heading down to the garage, I realized my first of many days to come with the Special Prosecutor was done. Leaving the FBI building, I felt certain David Gray had done a masterful job walking Rhee, Zelinsky, and Goldstein back off the ledge.

CHAPTER 5

We Regroup

THAT EVENING, THURSDAY, September 6, 2015, it was almost 6:30 p.m. EST when the FBI dropped us off at the Mayflower Hotel. David and I headed to our rooms, got out of our suits and ties, changed into business casual attire, and met in the lobby.

From the Mayflower lobby, we headed directly across the street to Casa de Monecristo by JR Cigar on L Street NW, where we bought some cigars. From there, we entered the building on the corner of Connecticut and L Street NW, went up the escalator, and ensconced ourselves in the smoking patio of Morton's Steakhouse.

I ordered a Martini. David got a vodka and tonic. We lit the cigars, ready to debrief what had just happened.

Since I did not have my cellphone, David called my wife for me and together we both briefed her on what had happened. She was relieved to know we were okay, but she was worried to learn the meeting had reached a rough spot and that we would have to come back to Washington to go through the ordeal all over again. Monica could see that even if this all turned out without me be being prosecuted for a crime, the family was going to be put through an ordeal—stress of a magnitude none of us had ever experienced before. If I ended up in federal prison, the family would be disrupted almost irreparably. A major source of family earnings would be gone. Even if I were not indicted and convicted of a crime, we were going to spend thousands of dollars with the Mueller investigation that we had not planned to spend.

After the phone call with Monica, David and I returned to debriefing one another. David explained that when he was asked out of the interview room, he found the prosecutors were angry and he knew his work was cut out for him. He began by asserting that when Zelinsky asked me to drive the interview, it was logical I went immediately for a conclusory statement in an attempt to bring the process to a quick close. Politely, David chided Zelinsky for giving up control of the interview to me, the subject of the investigation.

"I explained to Zelinsky that in all the law enforcement interrogations I have ever attended, I have never witnessed the head law enforcement investigator handing the investigation over to the witness," David explained. "We discussed some scholarly legal references on interrogation known to all lawyers and I argued to Zelinsky that his technique was unorthodox—an invitation for the interview to blow up in a disaster."

David also explained that I had not had an opportunity to review my 2016 emails because I wanted to preserve the state of both laptops at the time of the subpoena. He needed to refute the prosecutors' assertion that my memory was excellent, going back more than twenty years, so why wouldn't I remember my 2016 emails, especially emails this important?

"I told Zelinsky you get dozens of calls and hundreds of emails every week," David continued. "How could Zelinsky expect you to remember precisely every phone call and every email from two years ago?"

I suggested David should call Jay Sekulow and brief him on what had happened. David did so, moving to the other side of the outdoor patio so he could have a private conversation.

While I was alone, sitting there outside on Morton's patio with a cigar and a Martini on a beautiful late-summer, early-fall evening in D.C., the setting brought back memories of many similar evenings I had spent in the decades I had been for one reason or the other a constant visitor of the nation's capital. I have been in Washington under every president since Eisenhower.

The city has changed massively. Gone in downtown are most of the row houses and old but often glorious old stone buildings. The old city has been replaced by a new office building city where modern glass and chrome buildings all roughly nine-stories tall are built to hire the army of lobbyists, analysts, and political operatives that populate the city during the business day. I figured this trip would not be my last.

Reflecting on the day, I came to several conclusions.

- Number One: It was now clear to me that I was not a criminal target of the Mueller investigation. Had Mueller been out to prosecute me, Rhee had all she needed to charge me with perjury and offer a light sentence in return for cooperation. The first conclusion was that I was a subject of the investigation that Mueller wanted for testimony. Still, if Rhee, Zelinsky, and Goldstein were dissatisfied with the testimony I was giving, I was confident I would fall for a perjury trap that would lead to prison given the deficiencies in my precise memory of events two years earlier. The thought was chilling, and I felt genuine fear knowing I would have to face Mueller's prosecutors for a second round.

- Number Two: I began to contemplate the prosecutors were faced with a dilemma. If Mueller wanted me for testimony to indict and prosecute someone else, then the prosecutors could not charge me with perjury. How could I be a star witness if Mueller had charged me with perjury? The prosecutors had to take their pick. Charge me with making false statements to the FBI, or work with me and get the testimony Mueller needed—those seemed to be the choices Mueller would face in the final analysis.

- Number Three: I concluded that Roger Stone was Mueller's current target and that my testimony in regard to Stone was what Mueller needed to complete his criminal case against Stone. Clear to me now was that Mueller was still pursuing a Russian collusion theory and that he wanted to prosecute Stone for being the link between Trump and Assange. By indicting Stone, Mueller would build his case, working up the ladder, to his ultimate target—the impeachment of President Trump. I was the stepping stone Mueller planned to use to tie Stone to Assange. The logic would be that communications flowed from Assange to me to Stone, who in turn briefed Trump. That would make Stone the Trump operative who connected the candidate to Assange.

- Number Four: It was also clear to me that Rhee, Zelinsky, and Goldstein had decided to use the perjury trap as a means to pressure me that saved them from actually prosecuting me to get the same result. In other words, putting me on notice that I could now be charged with perjury, Rhee, Zelinsky, and Goldstein could calculate they now had the upper hand, trusting I would not make the same mistake twice. But I also realized how precarious my situation was. If a statement like I had made, which reflected my best current memory of why I didn't contact Assange could anger the prosecutors, then I concluded their patience was razor thin. How would I know if any memory I had could not be challenged by some "fact" they had gathered from an email, a text message, or a phone conversation? The prosecutors had a huge volume of data about me, and I was certain their goal was to question me under constant threat of perjury as if I remembered that data as precisely as they could document.

- Number Five: Finally, I concluded that while my willingness to cooperate was appreciated by the prosecutors, it was likely the prosecutors already had everything I handed over, plus more.

The only device I thought might be a plus to the prosecutors was the Time Machine. The Time Machine would contain a precise record of the laptop I had used throughout 2016, with all emails preserved in real time—including emails I might have deleted at one time or another during that year. My guess was that the prosecutors, with their unlimited resources in money, time, and personnel, probably knew more about me than I did.

When David got back to the table, he briefed me on his discussion with Sekulow and the president's legal team , including our interaction with the Mueller investigation that day. David Gray had communicated to Sekulow the warning I wanted given to the president. We had to assume the Special Counselor would have everything. All emails, text messages, written notes, and phone records could be obtained by search warrant. It was possible to obtain actual transcripts or recordings of all phone calls intercepted by FISA court authorized electronic surveillance, or by the National Security Administration under what is known as a "Section 702" request. A "702" is the form used to make a request to the National Security Administration to retrieve for an FBI investigation any information gathered by electronic surveillance that may have been taken on a U.S. citizen who is suspected in a national security investigation involving foreigners. Since Mueller was investigating alleged Trump campaign collusion with Russians, it is possible Trump, Stone, various campaign officials, and possibly even me had been under NSA electronic surveillance.

I wanted the president warned NOT to give in-person verbal testimony to Mueller under any circumstances. I was now confident Zelinsky had the answers to all questions he asked me. The way Mueller's team played the perjury trap was that any demonstrative answer that varied from evidence in the Special Counselor's possession could be deemed a lie, even if the person being interrogated thought they were telling the truth.

I was confident Zelinsky and his team must have had emails, text messages, and/or phone conversations they could use to contradict my assertion that I did not want to contact Assange and that I did not want to convince others to contact Assange because I did not want to be under intelligence investigation. Knowing Trump, I was sure his free-wheeling style of answering questions would make him a perfect target of a perjury trap sting set by world-class investigators such as Rhee, Zelinsky, and Goldstein. Trump's memory appeared as unreliable and shifting as mine. If I were capable of self-justification, I knew Trump would be many times even more vulnerable.

As we finished our drinks, David received a request from Roger Stone's attorney, asking if David could give him a call.

Through dinner, David and I decided the best strategy was for us to adopt a "no comment" response with the media, even though Mueller's team had imposed no restriction upon us and we were free to speak.

From this, it followed we did not want to talk with Roger Stone's attorney, at least not now. We suspected with the number of leaks that seemed to plague the Mueller investigation, there would be no way we could keep secret under lawyer-client privilege the knowledge we were in discussions with Stone's legal team.

"Still, I do not want Roger interpreting our refusal to talk with his lawyer as an indication I've flipped on him," I cautioned David. "If Roger thinks I might be a liability to him, or that I might turn state's evidence against him, Roger could be tempted to try to communicate with me through the press."

I was worried Roger had already said too much, and I knew the Special Counselor's office was monitoring everything Roger said. "Mueller probably has all Stone's emails and phone calls," I speculated to David. "My guess is Mueller has Roger under electronic surveillance right now and I'm afraid Roger will think he can stage his defense in the press." That I thought would be impossible, given my certainty

Roger would underestimate the unimaginable legal powers of the Special Counsel's office and the thoroughness of their investigation.

I told David we needed to craft in a few words a careful response to Roger's attorney, letting them know that we were in a situation where it was unwise to speak with Roger's legal team now, but that was a tactical calculation designed to protect both Roger and me.

Since I was a child, I have been fascinated by Abraham Lincoln. There is a famous telegram Lincoln sent General Grant at the end of the Civil War. In April 1865, General Lee broke out of the siege of Petersburg outside Richmond, making a desperate mad dash across Virginia to escape as Grant had an open route to enter Richmond. Lee's hope was that the remnants of his army could march southwest into North Carolina to unite with Confederate forces under the command of General Joseph E. Johnson.

Lincoln and Grant had developed a cryptic shorthand way of communicating with each other, careful to disguise their messages in as few words as possible so as to defy Confederate spies that seemed to be everywhere in Civil War Washington. In a telegraph message now in the National Archives, General Grant sent a telegram to Lincoln on April 7, 1865 at 11 a.m. that said: "Gen. Sheridan says, 'If the thing is pressed, I think that Lee will surrender.'"

What Grant was asking was for permission to attack and kill Lee's army in retreat. Grant knew that for the Union troops this would be a turkey-shoot, resulting in the deaths of hundreds of Confederate troops. The result would be to leave families without a husband, a father, a son, or a brother in a cause Lee was certain to lose.

Lincoln's response was simple. He took a pencil and wrote on Grant's telegram the following response, "Let the <u>thing</u> be pressed. A. Lincoln." Lincoln underlined the word "thing," a reference both he and Grant left unspecified. I had no doubt, given that what happened next, General Grant understood Lincoln approving the "thing" meant he had permission to kill retreating, hungry, and tired Confederate troops as if they were victims in a turkey shoot. Lincoln was willing to create this additional violence at the end of a horrific war if that is what it took to bring the war to a close.

Two days later, on April 9, 1865, Grant met with Lee at the home of Wilmer McLean in the village of Appomattox Courthouse. In a two-and-a-half hour meeting, Lee surrendered on terms Lincoln had quietly dictated to Grant and Sherman on March 27, 1865, at their private meeting at Grant's headquarters in City Point, Virginia, a few miles outside Richmond.

What David and I at dinner that night decided to communicate to Stone's attorney in response was this: "We decline, for now." That simple four word answer made clear our refusal to talk with Stone's attorney was calculated—a decision we planned to reverse when we felt we could do so safely. I was sure Roger would get the message and that Mueller, if the message were intercepted, would realize that by declining to work with Stone's attorney for now, we were still working with the Special Counselor's office in good faith.

The Special Counselor's office would also get the message our good faith was only for now. If the Special Counselor's office, and especially Aaron Zelinsky, should decide to play thug by threatening us again with a perjury trap, that good faith on my part could evaporate very quickly. From the beginning, I had never stopped thinking about blasting the Special Counsel in the press over their grilling me for what amounts in my mind to nothing more than politics. I had not been accused of committing any crime, yet here I was with my career interrupted, and here I was spending thousands of dollars defending myself. After nearly two years of failing, Mueller's team was still trying to prove the no evidence Russian collusion theory and my contact with Stone was under microscopic criminal examination.

The next day, Friday, September 7, 2018, we were free to leave Washington, since my appearance before the grand jury had been postponed. That morning, David decided he would drive back to New Jersey, planning to be home with his family for the weekend.

I decided to stay in Washington until Saturday morning.

The Mueller team promised to get my cellphone back to me on Friday morning, saying they also thought the FBI could return my MacBook Pro laptop and the external drive by Friday afternoon. I thought it was worth the extra day in D.C. if I could get my laptop back and get a jump on the process of restoring my computer to an end-2016 date by transferring data from the Time Machine. I was beginning to realize that the only chance I had to remember 2016 with any precision Mueller's prosecutors would demand was to examine the documentary record to see if I could reconstruct my activities during the 2016 presidential campaign.

But I was also worried that reviewing the emails would also trigger contradictory memories. I was worried that there was so much data in my election year emails that my head would spin trying to reduce it to "facts" for prosecutors who demanded everything be seen in black and white, while refusing to accept the possibility of gray. Not only could you not lie to the FBI, you could not forget something you preferred to forget. It was equally a crime to use "forgetting" as a tactic to hide evidence. With as much as I had forgotten over the past two years, I doubted I could remember enough to convince the prosecutors that I was not just "forgetting" conveniently.

CHAPTER 6

A Hard Rain Falling

THE NEXT DAY, Friday, September 7, 2018, David left the Mayflower early, wanting to get home to New Jersey with part of the working day still available once he arrived.

David called me from the road to tell me the FBI was expecting to bring my cellphone back to me this morning at 10:00 a.m. EST, and that they hoped to have my MacBook Pro and the Time Machine back by early afternoon.

At precisely 10:00 a.m. EST, Agent Jones, one of the two agents who served the subpoena at my home, called my room from the lobby. I told him I was in Room 525 and I invited him to come upstairs to deliver the phone back to me.

Agent Jones arrived with a second FBI agent, again confirming the FBI on missions in the field like this always work in teams. I invited the agents into the room. Both agents were extremely polite. When I did not recognize him at first, Agent Jones reminded me he was one of the two agents who came to my home to deliver the subpoena and that both he and Agent Smith had attended Thursday's interview with the Special Counsel's team. Agent Jones handed me my cellphone and got out the paperwork we needed to sign for me to confirm the cellphone had been returned. The second agent stood by the door and observed me signing the necessary paperwork, with a mission I was sure to monitor my demeanor and report back formally what he saw.

Before the two agents left, I told Agent Jones there was something I wanted to say. Agent Jones reminded me it might be better not to say anything until my lawyer was present. I persisted, insisting I wanted to say this anyway. "If the FBI has anything that could help me jog my memory, I would greatly appreciate the FBI sharing that information with me," I said, commenting that my only goal was to tell the truth. "When I get back to the office," Agent Jones replied, "we intend to put our heads together to see if there is anything that we can share with you." I thanked Agent Jones and the two FBI agents left as professionally as they had arrived.

The first call I made was to Monica, then to David. I let them both know I had my cellphone back. I left the Mayflower to take a walk on Connecticut Avenue, with a plan to get a late breakfast on L Street. Shortly after noon, David called and said the FBI was getting my laptop back from Quantico and their plan was to return it to me by 2:30 p.m. EST. At precisely 2:30 p.m. EST, an FBI agent called my hotel room from the lobby. I invited the FBI to come to the room. Two FBI agents that I had not previously seen knocked at the hotel room door a few minutes later. We went through the paperwork exercise and they both left, again politely, but this time without any conversation about the case.

I immediately set to work, plugging in the laptop and Time Machine at the desk in my hotel room. I had retired this laptop in 2017, largely because I was having trouble booting the computer and keeping it from crashing as I was working on it. It took almost two hours going through repeated efforts to boot the computer before I finally got it working. Next, I had to figure out how to restore the computer to an earlier date from the memory stored in the external drive. What I wanted to load was the last Time Machine save from the end of 2016. It took me until 6:00 p.m. EST to stabilize the computer and begin the restore. The restore software said it would take five hours to complete the download. I decided to head to Morton's.

Going down to the Mayflower lobby, I found Washington was being deluged by a hard, driving rain. After a few minutes studying the rain, I concluded the downpour was not going to stop soon and it was impossible to walk the two blocks to Morton's without getting drenched. In this tempest, there was no alternative except to take a cab. I tipped the doorman generously and got into a cab. "I will pay you twenty dollars to take me over to the Morton's Steakhouse across the street," I told the taxi driver. He agreed, heading to the first light where he made a U-turn to head down Connecticut Avenue in the direction of the White House. A block and a half later, he pulled up in front of the building in which Morton's was on the second floor. I paid the cab driver twenty dollars, as promised—he was delighted to be so well paid—and I ran inside, getting only moderately wet from the downpour.

At Morton's, I found the smoking patio looked like a flood scene. The rain had been so hard and steady, the drainage system couldn't handle the flow. I surveyed the patio to find a table by the door that was relatively dry. Still, the transparent plastic awnings the restaurant uses to keep out rain in the summer and cold in the winter were a failing barrier, flapping in the wind and unable to hold off the rain.

The truth is that I enjoy thunderstorms and heavy rains.

In Italy in late July and early August 2016 with Monica and family to celebrate our twenty-fifth wedding anniversary, I startled the hotel staff at the restaurant of the Grand Hotel Plaza, where we were staying by remaining in an outside restaurant through a similar hard rain falling. Through that storm in Italy, while other patrons and eventually the family headed inside, I remained in the outdoor patio, finishing dinner and enjoying a last glass of wine. All around the table, ultimately the only table still occupied by a patron, the outdoor restaurant suffered similar flooding. A wild thunder and lightning storm that created a flash flood in the town blew in from the mountains to pound the picturesque Lake Garda and the surrounding town, Lago di Garda.

I lit a cigar (which was not easy to do given the wind on the patio) and ordered a Martini. I realized I was one of the few patrons crazy enough to brave being outside during a storm of this magnitude. In between taking orders and delivering drinks, the patio staff scrambled madly to sweep the water off the patio floor to fight back the flooding.

Truthfully, it was foolhardy to remain outside during the deluge, but I enjoyed it and smoking was against the law inside the restaurant. After my second Martini, I went inside and ordered a steak. Before I left the patio, I gave Danny, the waiter who had served me at Morton's patio for years, a nice tip (on top of the tip I left with the drinks). Danny, who was then exhausted by the combined duress of serving the few crazy patrons like me who stayed outside during the rainstorm, and were simultaneously trying to fight back the water. "That's my hazard pay for the night," Danny thanked me gratuitously.

In the sixty-plus years that I have been in and out of Washington, the storm that night was the worst I had ever seen in the capital city. Reflecting on that, I decided the storm was an omen of the ordeal I was undergoing with the Special Counsel. Sitting outside in the middle of that rain storm, I kept hearing mentally Bob Dylan's classic 1962 ballad, "A Hard Rain's a'Gonna Fall." That night, to me, the roomful of "men with hammers" were the prosecutors. After this first encounter, I began their goal was not precisely to find the truth, but to convict Roger Stone. I knew Rhee, Zelinsky, and Goldstein were all Democrats. I felt the most fiercely partisan of the three was Zelinsky. And I knew this night sitting in that tempest, that a hard rain was going to fall, not just literally here, this night in Washington, D.C., but also, in my life.

In my lifetime, the political left in the United States has moved hard left. John Kennedy, if here were alive today, would be considered a tax-cutting conservative. These Democrats were ideologues. It's not just that the ideological left had moved socialist. It's also that the socialist Democrats proceed with an ideological fervor that casts small government, Constitutional conservatives as their political opponents. Today the hard left sees us as evil, deserving of imprisonment, censorship, and possibly even death. I feared the hard left in the United States was careening dangerously toward a Maoist-style cultural revolution that risked eliminating a generation of U.S. conservative intelligentsia.

This was shaping up rapidly to be one of the most stressful trials in my life. And I realized that all I had done was to work politically to get Donald Trump elected president. But David Gray was right. "Look in your rear-view mirror," David said to me at the start of all this. "There's a lot of corpses of Democratic politicians in your wake. These guys would love to put you in prison." David Gray, once again, was perceptive and right.

Still, I was encouraged to think I had been safe during the storm and that I was about to go inside for a steak dinner. The decision to stay in a comfortable hotel like the Mayflower, where I was a repeat guest over decades, and to eat every night in a restaurant where I was also considered a "regular" seemed at that moment a comfortable and safe decision. The staff at both places, recognizing me, always provided me privacy, while accommodating cheerfully my eccentricities. The only person missing was my dear wife Monica. She stayed back in New Jersey to continue running her business and to steer the ship with the family in my absence.

It was about 10:30 p.m. EST and it had quit raining when I left Morton's to walk back to the Mayflower. In my hotel room, I found the Time Machine had successfully restored the laptop to the condition it was in at the end of 2016. When it came time to reload the emails, I found I had over sixty-thousand emails in my computer at the end of 2016. I was overwhelmed. How possibly could I remember thousands of emails that I had not seen in two years? It was midnight, according to my detailed contemporaneous notes, before I began examining my emails.

Before I went to sleep, I found a critical email Roger Stone had sent me on July 25, 2016. The email was from Roger Stone to me and it was sent at 2:05 p.m. EST. The email was entitled "Get to Assange." In the text, Stone said, "At the Ecuadorian Embassy in London and get the pending WikiLeaks emails…they deal with

SILENT NO MORE

[Clinton] Foundation, allegedly." At 3:11 p.m. EST, I forwarded the email to Ted Malloch in London with a very simple message: "Ted. From Roger Stone. Jerry." I was in effect instructing Malloch to go to the Ecuadorian Embassy in London to see Julian Assange, founder and CEO of WikiLeaks, to find out what additional DNC emails Assange had. Please recall that on July 22, 2016, WikiLeaks had begun dropping over two days prior to the weekend delegates were arriving for the national nominating convention some 44,053 DNC emails that exposed Hillary Clinton and Debbie Wasserman Schultz colluding to smear Bernie Sanders and deny him the Democratic Party nomination for president.

As background, please understand Ted Malloch at that time was a professor and senior fellow in Management Practice at the Saïd Business School at the University of Oxford in the U.K. I met Ted in 2015 when research I was conducting on the Clinton Foundation with the assistance of New York expert investment analyst Charles Ortel, a long-time friend and associate of mine in New York City. I was about to raise question, based largely on Ortel's research, that Pricewater-houseCoopers, the multinational accounting and consulting firm, had conducted some questionable audits of the Clinton Foundation. I wanted to warn the international CEO of PWC before I put the research allegations in print. Jeffrey Mamorsky, another business associate who as a partner at the prestigious law firm Greenberg Trauig, LLP was one of the nation's top experts on ERISA law. Mamorsky put me in touch with Professor Theodore Roosevelt Malloch because Malloch for years had run a series of seminars bringing the international head of PWC together with Fortune 500 CEOs and their counterparts around the world.

Ted Malloch is a U.S. citizen who is a direct descendent of President Theodore Roosevelt. Malloch was born to a blue-blood family in Philadelphia.

He has a world-class resumé, having worked as a research professor at Yale and a senior fellow at Oxford. Malloch also served on the

73

executive board of the World Economic Forum at Davos, Switzerland, has held an ambassadorial level post in the United Nations, has worked in international capital markets on Wall Street, and has served in senior policy positions at the U.S. Senate Committee on Foreign Relations and in the State Department. Despite having the background of a globalist, Malloch is a Christian who defends U.S. sovereignty. Malloch's academic specialty involves research and teaching on the wisdom of applying Judeo-Christian principles to guide business ethics. Subsequent to the phone call over PWC, I flew to London and met with Malloch in 2015. Ultimately, I was responsible for publishing Malloch's autobiography with WND books.[24] Malloch and I have developed a close working relationship and friendship since then.

After meeting Roger Stone in February 2016, I arranged a dinner in New York City with Roger and Ted Malloch, a strong supporter of Donald Trump, for the next time both were in New York City at the same time. Malloch was anxious to assist the Trump campaign and he hoped Stone could arrange to have him appointed to Trump's presidential advisory staff—a hope that never materialized.

At the Mayflower Hotel, after discovering the Roger Stone email of July 25, I understood why the Special Counsel had accused me of lying. In my notes that evening, I wrote: "I had totally forgotten about this email." I underlined that sentence. My notes continued: "Clearly, I did not 'shut the door on Roger Stone's efforts to contact Julian Assange. Though I did not instruct Ted to follow through with this instruction—I did not instruct Ted 'Important' or 'Please Do ASAP'—I would not have forwarded the email to Ted unless I wanted Ted to follow through with the instruction. My conclusion today is that while I was not taking steps personally to contact Assange, I was okay with Malloch contacting Assange. Three days after this email, on

24   Malloch, Theodore Roosevelt. *Davos, Aspen, and Yale: My Life Behind the Elite Curtain as a Global Sherpa* (Washington, D.C.: WND Books, 2016).

Thursday, July 28, Monica and I with family left for Italy to celebrate our twenty-fifth wedding anniversary.

Roger Stone's email was one of some dozen emails that I responded to on July 25, 2016. It had been a very busy day that included writing an article in WND.com on George Noory's new novel *Night Talk*.[25] I was preparing for my appearance for a couple of hours on Noory's nationally syndicated radio show "Coast to Coast AM, an appearance that was scheduled to start at 1:00 a.m. EST that night. At around midnight, I sent David Gray an email with this July 25 email from Stone. I wanted David to know right away that there was a lot in my 2016 emails that I had forgotten.

This was further confirmed when I found an email chain that was started by Joseph Farah on August 10, 2016, while Monica and I were in Italy. Farah titled the email "Julian Assange Interview" and he was obviously upset that no one on the WND staff had managed to get in contact with Assange. From Italy, I responded to Farah: "I'm back in the United States on Friday. We can reach Assange, but someone may have to go to London. I'm sure if we went to the embassy [the Ecuadorian Embassy in London], he would talk to us." Here it became clear to me that my resistance to contacting Assange could have been overcome if Farah had made the assignment part of my job. Farah never purchased the airplane ticket and I never contacted Assange even though I had been in London twice while Assange was taking asylum in the Ecuadorian Embassy. The truth is I realized it would not be a crime for me to contact Assange.

Under the Pentagon Papers Supreme Court case, *New York Times Co. v. United States*, 403 U.S. 713 (1971), under the First Amendment, it was not a crime for a newspaper to publish stolen classified government information, provided the newspaper did not steal the information from the government. Democratic National Committee

---

25   Noory, George. *Night Talk* (New York: A Forge Book published by Tom Doherty Associates, LLC, 2016).

emails in Assange's possession obviously were stolen, but neither I nor WND had participated in the theft. I knew this because in 1972 I had written my political science dissertation as the final requirement to get my Ph.D. on a First Amendment topic. Inspired by the Pentagon Papers controversy, my dissertation was entitled "Prior Punishment, Prior Restraint, and Political Dissent: A Moral and Legal Evaluation."

My two dissertation advisers were at the opposite ends of the political spectrum: Professor Michael Walzer, a professor in the Political Science Department who was well-known as a socialist student of revolutionary politics, and Arthur E. Sutherland, Jr., a conservative emeritus law professor who was also one of the most respected historians of the Harvard Law School. That morning, when Michael Walzer drove me to my dissertation defense exam at Professor Sutherland's home in Cambridge, Massachusetts, I learned Sutherland had terminal cancer and I was to be his last dissertation candidate. Sutherland insisted I get the highest possible grade for my dissertation—an honor for which I have since been eternally grateful.

Going to sleep in the Mayflower Hotel late that night, I realized more precisely than ever just how fallible my memory truly is. What I told the Special Counsel about my reluctance to see Assange was not a lie, but it did reflect that after two years I was incapable of "remembering" events like I wanted to remember them. I knew that night that I would have to spend the next week downloading thousands of emails out of the Time Machine, so I could more accurately reconstruct what I did and said during the 2016 presidential election campaign.

Before leaving the Mayflower Hotel to take Amtrak back home to New Jersey the next day, Saturday, September 8, 2018, I telephoned Verizon and paid $160 to get the records of all my phone calls since January 1, 2016. While Monica had kept phone bills back through 2016 in our tax records, Verizon some time ago discontinued the practice of sending out print bills that list individual phone calls. I knew that in addition to my emails, I would have to reconstruct my telephone calls in 2016 in order to increase my odds of answering the Special Counsel's questions accurately. Sadly, Verizon refunded most the money, after informing me that the only way I could get a record of my phone calls back to 2016 was to get a court order. But I am not law enforcement and I had no way to compel Verizon to produce for me my own phone call records.

This was a futile effort. Verizon finally refused to give me my call-by-call phone records for 2016, unless I could get a search warrant or other form of court order to demand Verizon produce the records from archives. Verizon was not helpful. I found I had no alternative but to face the Special Counsel without being able to examine my phone records for 2016. But I had signed over to Mueller's team my consent for the prosecutors to obtain my Verizon phone records. To my dismay, Rhee, Zelinsky, and Goldstein refused to allow me or David Gray to have access to my Verizon call records from 2016 which it turns out they managed to obtain.

CHAPTER 7

The Exercise Remembering 2016

OUR SECOND MEETING with the Special Counsel's office was scheduled for Monday, September 17, 2018.

In deference to the spirit of working with the Special Counsel, I had suspended my live stream daily internet news broadcasts on CorsiNation.com since my birthday, August 31, 2018. This was another move that hurt my income while my expenses were mounting alarmingly fast dealing with Mueller and his team. Thankfully, the volunteer staff that assisted me in building the website and launching the daily live stream broadcasts worked together in my absence. I was truly proud of their dedication and abilities to continue in my absence. My work preparing to go back to the Special Counsel for a second interview had become full-time and all-consuming.

I spent most of the week reviewing my 2016 emails to reconstruct as best I could remember my activities throughout the final year of the presidential election campaign. I gave particular attention to my interaction with Roger Stone. When I downloaded the Time Machine, I was astounded to find there were over sixty-four thousand emails on my MacBook Pro laptop as of the end of December 2016. With that volume of email traffic, it was no wonder I could not distinctly remember individual emails without studying the email file to refresh my memory. As I read the emails, I began to develop a vague recollection that while I was in Italy, I knew that Assange and WikiLeaks were saving Podesta emails for their next email drop on the Democrats. I could not remember how I came to know this, but I was beginning to feel certain that I did.

We had returned from Italy on Friday, August 12, 2016. On Monday, August 15, 2016, I published an article in WND.com titled "Trump Advisor: WikiLeaks Plotting Email Dump to Derail Hillary."[26] In my draft of that article, I acknowledged in the first paragraph that Roger Stone had told me he was in contact with Julian Assange, but presumably through a source other than me. While I recall telling Stone in August 2016 that Assange had Podesta emails that he planned to drop serially in October, I do not recall that I told Stone I got that information either directly from Assange or indirectly through an intermediary. My recollection has remained constant: namely, that I just connected the dots and figured out for myself what Assange was planning to do next.

The first paragraph of the draft article read:

In an exclusive interview with WND, Roger Stone, the co-author of the best-selling book "The Clintons' War on Women" and a longtime friend of Donald Trump, detailed the extent to which his computer system and bank accounts have been hacked after he established contact with Julian Assange of Wikileaks.

The second paragraph in the draft article continued the theme:

Stone explained to WND he believes the hack was in retaliation for Stone's recent media interviews in which he has revealed he believes Assange has a complete set of Hillary Clinton's 30,000 scrubbed "private emails," believes involved communications with Clinton's State Department aides Cheryl Mills and Huma Abedin and is preparing for a strategic release of these emails designed to derail Clinton's 2016 presidential campaign.

---

26   Corsi, Jerome R. "Trump Adviser: WikiLeaks Plotting Email Dump to Derail Hillary," WND.com, August 15, 2016. *https://www.wnd.com/ 2016/08/trump-adviser-wikileaks-plotting-email-dump-to-derail-hillary/.*

This suggested that what I told Stone about Assange holding Podesta emails for subsequent release, Stone had taken possibly as conjecture or speculation on my part that the remaining DNC emails that Assange had yet to publish were Podesta's. From this article, it did not appear that Stone had concluded I knew for certain what Assange was going to do next. Stone had listened to my prediction, but it appears he did not accept as actual fact-certain that I knew for sure.

In my notes made on rediscovering this article, I wrote, "This article published on August 15, 2016 makes clear that by that date I believed Stone had succeeded in contacting Assange through a source that did not involve me." My notes also reflect that I realized if Stone had contacted Assange it must have been since July 25, 2016, just before we left for Italy, when Stone was urging me to get in touch with Assange—a message I passed the message onto Ted Malloch. My guess was that if Stone were telling the truth, he must have contacted Assange while I was in Italy, between July 25 and August 15, 2016.

Yet, looking at the article more closely I concluded that on August 15, 2016, Stone was stuck on incorrect information. Stone then apparently believed Assange was yet to publish information on the Clinton Foundation, information he appeared to believe would to be found in the much sought-after thirty-thousand missing Hillary Clinton emails that she had withheld as "private" and "personal." While Stone was not listening to me, I wondered who the source Stone was believing.

With information published recently in 2018 by the Daily Caller, I finally discovered that Stone had claimed he had a second source to be in contact with Assange. On July 25, 2016, the same day Stone had sent me the "Get to Assange" email that I forwarded to Malloch, Stone had been blind-copied on an email exchange between my New York investment analyst friend Charles Ortel and James Rosen, who at that time was a reporter for Fox News. On that day, Rosen emailed Ortel, "Am told WikiLeaks will be doing a massive dump of HRC emails relating to the CF (Clinton Foundation) in September."[27] I continue to suspect that Stone had other sources that provided him access to Assange and WikiLeaks.

So, evidently, on July 25, 2016, Stone had what he considered good inside information about WikiLeaks and Assange from Rosen, but he still wanted me to check it out. This must have prompted me to try to figure it out. In early August 2016, when I explained my conclusion Assange had Podesta emails, Stone must have concluded I was answering his question, but since I still lacked a link to Assange, Stone decided to go with what Rosen had told him—namely that the DNC emails that Assange was holding to drop later (in September, according to Rosen) would be Hillary Clinton emails involving the Clinton Foundation.

Clearly, Rosen had the month wrong. The next drop of DNC emails began on October 7, 2016, not September. Rosen also had wrong which DNC emails Assange had saved to drop in October 2016—it turned out to be the Podesta emails, not specifically DNC emails relating to the Clinton Foundation. But evidently Stone took as more authoritative Rosen's inside knowledge, which Rosen's email to Ortel suggested came from WikiLeaks directly or from a Rosen source that was in direct touch with Assange. At any rate, my conclusion was that when I shared with Stone in August 2016 my conclusion Assange would drop Podesta's emails in October, I did not tell Stone I had gotten that information either directly from Assange, or from an intermediary source I may have had that was in direct touch with Assange. My second conclusion is that when I shared my conclusions with Stone in early August, he was not sure I was right.

On August 15, 2016, at 4:51 p.m. EST, I sent an email to Roger Stone allowing him to see a pre-publication draft of my article. He

---

27   Enjeti, Saagar. "Exclusive: Roger Stone Says Wikileaks Claim Was Based in Part on Reporter's Email," The Daily Caller, October 22, 2018 *https:// dailycaller.com/2018/10/22/roger-stone-wikileaks-claim-reporter-email/*.

did not email with any suggested changes. My draft title for the article was: "Trump Ally Hacked After Revealing WikiLeaks Julian Assange Plans Email Drops on Clinton Foundation." The point of the article was that Stone believed his computer and personal bank accounts were hacked in retaliation for publicly declaring Assange had a complete set of Hillary Clinton's scrubbed thirty thousand "private emails" and was planning to release them to derail the Democratic Party nominee's presidential campaign. WND editor Art Moore properly moved that paragraph to the lead of the article. The edited article was published by WND.com on August 15, 2016, at 7:36 p.m. EST.

On Tuesday, August 16, 2016, I sent Ted Malloch an email in the U.K., asking if he could find Bernie Sanders' brother who was in the U.K. at that time. My email to Malloch continued: "He (Bernie Sanders' brother) is on the record saying he plans to vote for Trump. Roger Stone suggested you might track down Sanders' brother." This was the third request Stone made of Malloch. At dinner in New York City when I introduced Roger to Ted, Roger asked Ted to research Bill Clinton's time as a Rhodes Scholar at Oxford. Roger believed Bill Clinton had been dismissed from the program because Clinton had raped a female graduate student at Oxford. Then, on July 25, 2016, I passed Roger's email on to Ted, asking Ted to go see Assange in London. Ted waned an advisory position with the Trump campaign and Stone believed Malloch could improve his chances by scoring on one of these three requests. To the best of my recollection, Ted never said anything to me to suggest he had succeeded on any of the three requests.

On August 21, 2016, Stone published his famous prediction on Twitter: "It will soon be Podesta's time in the barrel." This has subsequently been widely interpreted as proof Stone had advanced knowledge that the DNC emails Assange had yet to publish were those of John Podesta, at that time the chair of Hillary Clinton's presidential campaign. This is the central email that had become the focus of the Special Counselor's criminal investigation into Roger Stone. The hypothesis of the Special Counselor evidently was that Roger

Stone was the link between Julian Assange and Donald Trump that was essential if the Trump campaign's alleged collusion with Russia to win the 2016 presidential election were to be proved. Again, I suspected found another link to Assange that affirmed my original early August prediction.

On Tuesday, August 30, 2016, Stone emailed me, saying "Please call me." At 5:59 p.m. EST that day, I emailed Stone the following reply: "Will do. Just got back to New Jersey from New York City. Give me a few minutes." I have no precise recollection of that phone call. But from what happened next, I have reconstructed that in the phone call Stone told me he was getting heat for his tweet and needed some cover. Writing cover stories is standard operating procedure for consultants in political campaigns, with the goal of providing alternative explanations to mask what could otherwise be politically damaging narratives or uncomfortable but costly facts. I had begun researching the millions of dollars John Podesta and Hillary Clinton had made selling U.S. military technology to Russia, including the hypersonic missile technology that Russia used to develop a hyper-sonic nuclear ICBM that could defy the U.S. "space wars" anti-missile defense system created first under the Reagan administration. This, I believed would make an excellent cover-story for Stone's unfortunate tweet.

On July 31, 2016, Peter Schweizer, president of the Government Accountability Institute based in Washington, D.C., a trusted associate of mine over many years, wrote an article in the Wall Street Journal that raised the question, "Why did Hillary's State Department urge U.S. investors to fund Russian research for military uses?"[28]

The next day, August 1, 2016, the Government Accountability Institute published a research report titled "From Russia with

---

28   Schweizer, Peter. "The Clinton Foundation, State and Kremlin Connections," *Wall Street Journal,* July 31, 2016. *https://www.wsj.com/articles/the-clinton-foundation-state-and-kremlin-connections-1469997195.*

Money: Hillary Clinton, the Russian Reset, and Cronyism."[29] The report contained evidence a Putin-connected Russian government fund transferred $35 million dollars to a small company with John Podesta on its executive board, which included several senior Russian officials. That is when I began extensive research on John Podesta and his financial connections to Russia—connections I found to be both extensive and highly suspicious, especially since I had evidence Podesta had been receiving payoffs in stock via a shell corporation in the Netherlands that the Panama Papers on off-shore transactions had targeted as an entity Russia had used to launder money.

In my late evening telephone call with Stone on August 30, 2016, I suggested Stone could use me as an excuse, claiming my research on Podesta and Russia was the basis for Stone's prediction that Podesta would soon be in the pickle barrel. I knew this was a cover story, in effect not true, since I recalled telling Stone earlier in August that Assange had Podesta emails that he planned to drop as the "October Surprise," calculated by Assange to deliver a knock-out blow to Hillary Clinton's presidential aspirations.

On my birthday, August 31, 2016, I emailed Stone at 4:49 p.m. EST a nine-page background memorandum on John Podesta that I had written that day at Stone's request. I couched the Podesta background paper as a rejoinder Stone could use to counter a report CNN published August 15, 2016, titled "Manafort named in Ukrainian probe into millions in secret cash."[30] The CNN article highlighted the FBI had begun an investigation of former Trump campaign chairman Paul Manafort for his financial dealings regarding

---

29   "From Russia with Money: Hillary Clinton, the Russian Reset, and Cronyism," Government Accountability Institute, August 1, 2016. https://www.g-a-i.org/wp-content/uploads/2016/08/Report-Skolkvovo-08012016.pdf.

30   Wright, David. "Manafort named in Ukrainian probe into millions in secret cash," CNN Politics, Aug. 15, 2016. https://www.cnn.com/2016/08/15/politics/clinton-slams-trump-over-manafort-report/index.html.

the consulting he had conducted for former Ukraine president Victor Yanukovych.

At Roger's request, after a telephone conversation in March 2017 that I vaguely recall from memory—I have no recording or notes from the conversation—Roger asked me to write an article how he got his information for his Twitter post on August 21, 2016. Roger and I agreed once again that the tweet was unspecific as to why Stone believed Podesta would be in the pickle barrel. That allowed us once again to roll out the cover story that Stone based his comment on background information I provided Stone from public source materials on Podesta's financial dealings in Russia while Hillary was secretary of state.

On March 22, 2017, I drafted for Roger an article ultimately published in Infowars.com that my notes show I titled, "'Blame Me!' Corsi says. 'Not Assange.'" Here is how the article began:

> *Roger Stone is under attack by the Democrats in Congress for a tweet he posted on Aug. 21, 2016, in which Stone said, "Trust me, it will soon the [be] Podesta's time in the barrel."*

> *Democrats seeking to charge, have mistakenly used this email to "prove" Stone had advance knowledge Julian Assange at Wikileaks was about to release emails hacked from John Podesta, then the chairman of Hillary Clinton's 2016 presidential campaign.*

> *Having reviewed my records, I am now confident that I am the source behind Stone's tweet.*

Stone used the cover story excuse again when he testified under oath to the House Intelligence Committee on September 26, 2017. In that testimony, Stone claimed his "pickle barrel" tweet was based on "a comprehensive, early August opposition research briefing provided to me by investigative journalist, Dr. Jerome Corsi, which I then asked him to memorialize in a memo that he sent me on August 31st, all of which was culled from public records." To stress the point, Stone attached to his testimony a copy of my background research memorandum on Podesta.[31]

To prepare for our second trip to Washington for our return interview with the prosecutors for the Special Counselor, David Gray had a preliminary telephone conference with prosecutors Aaron Zelinsky and Andrew Goldstein. David had fostered a relationship on our first visit in which he could mediate with the prosecutors, acting as a buffer between the prosecutors and me. Seeing that David was willing to play this role, the prosecutors began to share with David in advance the focus of their next round of questions. This was a tremendous advantage for us because the willingness of the prosecutors to intermediate through David allowed David and me to prepare to answer the specific concerns the prosecutors intended to raise in the next interview with me.

Zelinsky disclosed the prosecutors had specific evidence that after the July 25, 2016 "Get to Assange" memo from Stone to me, I had specific information, even while I was in Italy, that Assange had in his possession unpublished memos from John Podesta. Even more, Zelinsky, asserted my intelligence included that Assange planned to release the Podesta emails in October 2016, and when he did release the Podesta emails, Assange planned to do so in a "drip-by-drip" fashion. In other words, Zelinsky made clear that the prosecutors had demonstrable proof that I knew Assange had Podesta emails he would release in October a serial fashion, not all at once but over many days, to maximize the impact of the emails to influence the news cycle

---

31   Borchers, Callum. "Roger Stone's defiant congressional testimony on Trump and Russia, annotated," *Washington Post*, September 26, 2017. *https://www.washingtonpost.com/news/the-fix/wp/2017/09/26/roger-stones-defiant-congressional-testimony-on-trump-and-russia-annotated/?utm_term=.8c30c6849bff.*

against Hillary Clinton at the end of the election. We all understood that having advance knowledge like this of the detailed specifics of an impending "October Surprise" of sufficient magnitude to tip the election in Trump's favor would provide the Trump campaign with a major tactical advantage.

Zelinsky told David Gray the prosecutors could prove I shared this information from Italy, and afterwards, not only with Stone but with several other people. What astonished Zelinsky and the Special Counselor's prosecutorial team was how I had obtained information this accurate in July and August, months before Assange began dropping Podesta's emails on October 7, 2016. Zelinsky and the other prosecutors believed I had to have either direct contact with Assange myself, or I had to have a source who was in direct contact with Assange. Zelinsky argued that my advance information about Assange and the Podesta emails was so uncannily accurate that only Assange could have conveyed that information to me, either directly or through an intermediary.

According to David Gray's notes on the conversation, Zelinsky also said the prosecutors had evidence that I played a role in timing Assange's release of the Podesta emails to occur on October 8, 2016, to compete in the news cycle with the release of the Billy Bush tape.

On Friday, October 7, 2016, two days before the second presidential debate, the *Washington Post* reported the newspaper had obtained a video showing Donald Trump bragging "in vulgar terms about kissing, groping, and trying to have sex with women during a 2005 conversation caught on a hot microphone, saying that 'when you're a star, they let you do it.'"[32] While the newspaper did not disclose how the eleven-year-old video had been obtained, the "hot mic" video clearly captured Trump talking with Billy Bush, then host of "Access Hollywood" on a bus with the show's name written across the side, arriving on a Hollywood set to tape a segment with Trump. Billy Bush, a well-known radio and television host, is a member of the Bush family. Trump captured by the "hot mic" can be heard boasting about grabbing women by their sexual organs.

The timing of the release of the Billy Bush segment suggests the tape was calculated to be Democrats' "October Surprise" against Donald Trump. Political operatives like Roger Stone had realized from the start of the 2016 presidential campaign that capturing an increased share of female voters was a key strategy Trump needed to implement to win. This tape was certain to cost Trump votes among women voters nationwide—votes he could not afford to lose.

According to Politifact.com, the *Washington Post* published an article on the Billy Bush tape at approximately 4:00 p.m. EST on October 7, 2016.[33] Almost simultaneously, Wikileaks posted a tweet at 4:32 p.m., October 7, 2016, announcing the first publication of

---

32   Paquette, Danielle. "Why the most part of Donald Trump's 'hot mic' comments isn't the vulgar language," in "Wonkblog," *Washington Post*, October 7, 2016. *https://www.washingtonpost.com/news/wonk/ wp/2016/10/07/the-real-issue-with-donald-trump-saying-a-man-can-do- anything-to-a-woman/?utm_term=.f810e6607f63*. See also: Fahrenthold, David A. "Trump recorded having extremely lewd conversation about women in 2005," *Washington Post*, October 8, 2016. *https://www. washingtonpost.com/politics/trump-recorded-having-extremely-lewd- conversation-about-women-in-2005/2016/10/07/3b9ce776-8cb4-11e6- bf8a-3d26847eeed4_story.html?postshare=3561475870579757&ti d=ss_tw&utm_term=.3c9b54a632d2*.

33   Sharockman, Aaron. "It's True: WikiLeaks dumped Podesta emails hour after Trump video surfaced," Politifact.com, December 18, 2016. *https://www.politifact.com/truth-o-meter/statements/2016/dec/18/ john-podesta/its-true-wikileaks-dumped-podesta-emails-hour-afte/*.

the Podesta emails at 4:32 p.m. EST, October. 7, 2016. What makes the timing even more suspicious was that WikiLeaks had called off an event scheduled for the Ecuadorian Embassy in London on Tuesday, October 4, 2016, at which Assange was expected to release a new batch of emails mails that Assange had announced would contain damaging information on Hillary Clinton.

Zelinsky told David Gray that Stone had told me in advance about the Billy Bush video and asked me to get word to Assange to hold the release of the first batch of the Podesta emails until after the *Washington Post* had published the damaging Billy Bush "hot mic" recording.

Finally, Zelinsky revealed that after October 7, 2016, the prosecutors had evidence of an email exchange between Stone and me in which Stone expressed pleasure that Assange had released the Podesta emails as instructed, and in which I replied that Stone and I "should be given credit."

When David briefed me, I began to understand why the Special Counsel had waited to interview me after interviewing some thirty of Stone's associates. The way prosecutions approach investigations, the target of the investigation is interviewed last. Prosecutors typically move up the ladder, proceeding from the least important witnesses to the most important witnesses, ending up with the target at the top of the ladder.

What was clear to me now was that Rhee, Zelinsky, and Goldstein all were out to prove that I was the link between Assange and Stone—the key link to Assange that the prosecutors had to establish to advance their Russian collusion narrative. If no one from the Trump campaign had direct access to Assange, how could Robert Mueller possibly prove their Russian collusion narrative? Without this narrative fully proved, how could Mueller possibly indict Stone? In doing so, Rhee, Zelinsky, and Goldstein were all ignoring the fact that Roger consistently got wrong what Assange had. Stone did go public suggesting Assange would release Podesta emails next, but

Stone did not go forward with that until his "pickle barrel" tweet of August 21, 2016.

While David Gray could see no crime I had committed, he was sure the prosecutors were going to push me to name the source that put me in contact with Assange. The prosecutors had saved interviewing me until they had interviewed most of Stone's other important associates because I was obviously higher up on their ladder. Getting David's briefing before our second meeting with the Special Counselor, I appreciated more than ever that while I was not a target of the Special Counselor's investigation, Mueller wanted me as a key witness who the prosecutors felt could establish the link with Assange needed to finalize Mueller's Russian collusion case. I now had no doubt the prosecutors' narrative put the links to the release of Podesta's emails this way: from Assange to Corsi, from Corsi to Stone, and from Stone to Trump.

My problem was that I could remember no such person who attempted to put me in touch with Assange, or to act for me as a go-between with Assange. I still believed that I had never spoken to Assange and that I had not communicated with Assange through any intermediary.

I still believed I had concluded by deduction that Assange had Podesta emails that he would drop over a series of days in October 2016, framing what Assange believed would be the "October Surprise" that would cost Hillary the White House.

Going forward, I knew my inability to name a source who put me in touch with Assange was going to be a major sticking point with Mueller's prosecutors.

CHAPTER 8

Before the Grand Jury

I WAS SCHEDULED to appear before the Grand Jury on Friday, September 21, 2018, in Washington, D.C. What I experienced that week was pure hell.

David Gray and I had traveled back to Washington on Sunday, September 16, to be in Washington for the FBI to pick us up at the Mayflower Hotel for a scheduled 10:00 a.m. interview with the Special Prosecutor. While I felt somewhat more prepared, having had a chance to review my 2016 emails, I was certain my interrogation would intensify.

With David and I parked once again in the interrogation room with no windows, Jeannie Rhee, Aaron Zelinsky, and Andrew Goldstein filed into the room with their army of FBI agents for another "Duke It Out" session.

Almost immediately, Zelinsky launched into what I expected was the point on which this entire exercise was bound to fail.

"When you were in Italy on your twenty-fifth wedding anniversary, did you provide Roger Stone with information about Wikileaks?" Zelinsky asked pointedly.

"Yes, I believe I told Roger Stone that I thought Assange had Podesta's emails," I responded.

"Who was your source of information?" Zelinsky asked in an angry tone.

In the conversations David Gray had with the prosecutors in between meetings, David explained that I believed I had simply connected the dots, figuring out from open source information that

Assange had Podesta's emails, that Assange would release those emails as an "October Surprise," and that Assange would release the Podesta emails in a serial drip-by-drip fashion with WikiLeaks releasing new Podesta emails every day in October right up until the election.

The prosecutors replied to David what became the refrain they repeated over and over: "We have evidence that Doctor Corsi knew in August 2016 that Assange had Podesta's emails. We can prove that Corsi knew Assange would hold these emails until October 2016, and that he would release them drip-by-drip fashion over a series of days right up until the election is held."

David reported to me that Zelinsky used over and over again the legal phrase in Latin, "*Ad Seriatum,*" a term that in Latin means "one after the other." David said Zelinsky seemed very proud to make this pronouncement in Latin, as if the Latin made the pronouncement sound more official that, in his opinion, I had to be lying. Zelinsky insisted to David that there was no possible way I could have figured out Assange had Podesta's email with this degree of accurate pre-knowledge unless I had a source connected to Assange who told me Assange had Podesta's emails and how Assange planned to use them.

Over the next few hours, Zelinsky and Rhee would use any number of techniques to push me to remember a source. Finally, Zelinsky said, "Doctor Corsi, many people find they have to put themselves back in time to a particular date and place to remember precisely what happened." Zelinsky suggested I should go back to my trip to Italy, putting myself mentally back to July and August 2016.

I put my hand up to my forehead, closed my eyes, and tried to engage seriously in this regression exercise. "I think I see someone telling me about Assange," I finally said, trying hard to imagine myself in Italy talking about WikiLeaks.

"Was it a man or a woman?" Rhee asked, with obvious enthusiasm that the prosecutors may finally be breaking though a mental block they presumed I had.

"I think it was a man," I responded. Then, I realized how ridiculous this was. As I was beginning to invent people and make things up just to answer their persistent questions. But it really struck me as preposterous that a serious U.S. DOJ prosecutor like Zelinsky would ask me to use the type of regression technique used by hacks promising to unlock for gullible clients past-lives embellishments to enrich otherwise troubled present existences.

"I think if we continue this, I will be telling you that next I was Alexander the Great in a former life," I explained to Zelinsky.

Truthfully, Zelinsky's regression technique struck me as being worthy of a carnival trick and I wondered whether next Zelinsky would suggest putting me under hypnosis. I felt silly going through this carnival exercise in front of three of Mueller's top prosecutors and an army of FBI there to record my every word and to analyze my body language to tell if I was telling the truth or lying.

Repeatedly, Rhee and Zelinsky instructed me to "tell us the truth," followed by the instruction, "when you can't remember, just say that you can't remember."

But when I explained that my best recollection was that I had no source that linked me to Assange, all three prosecutors—Rhee, Zelinsky, and Goldstein—appeared to jump to the conclusion that I was lying. In other words, it did me no good to explain to them that my best recollection was that I figured out Assange had Podesta's emails and, although I may have had a source to Assange, I could not remember a source.

"Who are you protecting?" Rhee and Zelinsky joined in tag-team challenging me, with their intensity and anger rising at every question. "Are you protecting Roger Stone? Are you protecting Donald Trump?"

I told them that I was there voluntarily, and I was trying to work with the Special Prosecutor, but I would not lie to invent an answer they obviously wanted to hear.

The more this interrogation went on, the more confused I became.

At one point, Zelinsky decides to try regression techniques.

"Sometimes people remember when they regress themselves mentally back into a period of time," Zelinsky instructs me. "Try going back to 2016. Imagine yourself in Italy, communicating with Roger Stone about Assange."

The prosecutors have a whole list of people, including unrelated business contacts, that I was working with in 2016. One by one, I am questioned, "Did you tell this person what Assange had? How about that person?" After I surrendered my computers and my Time Machine, Mueller's investigation knew every person and company with whom I had a consulting contract, plus numerous professional contacts, like Wall Street investment analyst Charles Ortel, with whom I had undertaken since 2015 an investigation of Clinton Foundation financial scandals.

Finally, at the end of another grueling day of third-degree questioning, the FBI dropped us, completely exhausted, off at the Mayflower Hotel at about 6:00 p.m. EST. David and I packed up and headed back to New Jersey.

Zelinsky and Rhee were asking me very detailed questions about my activities in 2016, yet they refused to share with me the evidence they had. It soon became clear to me that even though I had restored the end of 2016 from the Time Machine to my MacBook Pro, I still did not have all my 2016 emails. Yet the prosecutors insisted on me answering questions when they had the full detail on emails about which I was being questioned and Mueller's team refused to allow me to see those emails before answering.

I still do not understand why Mueller insisted upon playing this stupid interrogation game worthy of the Gestapo, the KGB, or the Red Guard under Mao. Increasingly, I felt like I was a U.S. soldier captured in the Korean War being interrogated by the communist Chinese. All this lacked was the sleep deprivation, the torture beatings, and the blinding white interrogation that blocked me from seeing my inquisitors.

Whenever I tried to explain to Mueller's prosecutors and the FBI the context of their questions, Zelinsky or Rhee accused me of "trying to create a narrative." If I pursued whether this person or that person may have told me something, Mueller's prosecutors and the FBI accused me of lying, of giving them false information so as to mislead them. My pleas that I was just trying to figure out what happened in 2016 fell on deaf ears.

During one of the breaks when the prosecutors and the FBI were out of the room angry, I told David that I was being questioned as if I were a criminal, not like someone who was trying to help them. Mueller and the FBI had everything, including emails I did not have, complete phone call records that I had not seen because both Verizon and Mueller had refused to give them to me.

These "grand inquisitors"—a Dostoyevsky term I kept thinking about—expected me to have perfect recall the first time, even in response to their granular questions about events that happened two years ago. I was expected to have excellent recall of 2016 emails that the grand inquisitors would not allow me to see, so I might refresh my memory. And if I made the slightest mistake, got a name wrong, or forgot about somebody being at a meeting, the grand inquisitors put on angry faces and began yelling at me, in increasingly strident tones, reminding me I could be sent to prison for giving the FBI false information.

I told David this inquisition was reminding me of a game of twenty questions in which you committed felonies and could be imprisoned for false answers. I took up a yellow pad and said to David, "This nightmare is like a legal pad where Zelinsky holds the pad up to me, so I can see only one side, and he writes a number on the other side. I have to guess the number Zelinsky wrote otherwise I have lied to the FBI." My point was that I had to answer precisely to Mueller's team and the FBI about emails, documents, phone calls, and testimony where I was not allowed to see the evidence the grand inquisitors had.

I took David's legal pad, held one side up to him, and proceeded to demonstrate. "I'm writing a number on the other side that you can't see," I told David. "What is the number?" David guessed the number, "Eight."

When I turned the pad around, David could see that I had not written a number, instead I just went through the motions, so it looked like I was writing a number. "What's the point?" I asked David. "I came in here to cooperate, to help Mueller and the FBI figure out the evidence they might have. Instead, I'm being interrogated like a criminal."

I realized it was inevitable that I would fall for the perjury trap. The Mueller prosecutors and the FBI participating in the inquisition had gotten me to do so the first day, in the first hours. I realized that was a Mueller strategy trap. Once I had made a mistake of memory, Mueller had what he needed to prosecute me for the crime of lying to the FBI. This was done, I believe, so I would always feel the heat, so I would confess anything to Mueller that Mueller wanted. But I never had any intention of lying, so this stupid game was unnecessary. I have a history of telling the truth, even when the truth is not always in my favor.

When it was lunchtime, Mueller and the FBI put on their coats and went out for lunch. David and I did not want to leave the FBI building for fear of being seen and hounded by the press. So, I stayed in the conference room without windows while David searched to see if the building had a cafeteria. I spent countless hours in that interrogation room alone, while the Mueller team and the FBI walked out infuriated at some answer I had given, and David was called into a separate conference room to plead mercy and ask them to continue without arresting me on the spot.

Left alone for hours in the conference room, I did not have my cellphone. I did not have my laptop. I had no book to read. I was left to pace around that conference table for hours, alone but always aware the opaque electronic eye on the ceiling could well be broadcasting to FBI in another room who were observing and reporting on my every move. Wondering what was going on was driving me insane, worrying that my fate was being decided in the next room. Would I be arrested on the spot? Taken from this secret interrogation room to prison, handcuffed. Would David have to call my wife in New Jersey to tell her he was trying to get standing to practice law in Washington, so he could bail me out?

In a futile attempt to ease my anxiety, I used these hours left alone, prisoner in that interrogation room with no windows and a door through with I could not leave without being accompanied by the FBI (even to go to the restroom), I decided to count the number of light boxes recessed into the ceiling. I counted the number of carpet tiles there were on the floor.

I studied the two large conference tables in the room and discovered they did not match. Both tables were old, well used, most likely recovered from government surplus. The chairs around the conference table looked like they came from one set, but it was obvious the chairs too were used. I concluded the chairs came from a different office set that either of the two conference tables because the heavy scuff marks on the arms of the chair did not match how the chairs bumped into this set of two conference tables.

Driving home with David, I felt as if I might be experiencing what my parents had politely called a "nervous breakdown." I was a psychological mess and the worst part was that I knew we had to come back on Thursday for me to testify to the grand jury on Friday. I expected that experience to be even more terrifying. I was concluding that I should advise no U.S. citizen to ever talk to the FBI, even with an army of defense attorneys at the table.

The way the FBI plays this stupid grand inquisitor game violates all Constitutional freedoms. I was not being given a right to see evidence that was being used to incriminate me, if only because I tried to remember what the evidence was about, and I happened to remember imperfectly.

We had expected the prosecutors would want to interview us on Tuesday, or surely on Thursday before scheduled grand jury appearance on Friday.

But instead, the prosecutors told David that I was not needed until Friday morning. Left with the prospect of cooling our heals for several days in Washington with nothing particular to do, we decided we would return home.

Before returning to Washington for the Grand Jury, I made an appointment with my heart specialist. I have been under medical treatment for high blood pressure and hypertension for years. After a thorough examination, the physician prescribed a relatively mild sedative. The cardiologist advised me that I must rest and that the stress could trigger a stroke or a heart attack if I were not careful. He reminded me that at seventy-two years old, my body could not withstand the level of stress I have experienced even ten years ago, when I was detained in Kenya for going there in 2008 to investigate Obama's birth certificate.

Since meeting with my cardiologist, I have not been able to shake the increasing worry that under this much tension from Mueller, I could well have a heart attack or a stroke. I started finding it difficult to sleep. Around 10:00 p.m. each night, I found myself collapsing of exhaustion. But, after getting enough rest for my mind to become active again, I found myself coming fully awake at around 1:00 a.m. and unable to go to sleep for the rest of the night. My inability to sleep affected my wife, who began suffering sleep deprivation herself. Truly, dealing with Mueller had become a serious health problem for me and my wife together, especially with both of us in our senior years.

On Friday morning, September 21, 2018, the FBI took David and me to the Federal Courthouse in Washington. We entered the building through the basement and passed security screening in the garage. David and I were taken upstairs to a smaller inside conference room, adjoining the grand jury room. Here we were to meet with the prosecutors to prepare for the grand jury.

I understood that David would not be allowed to go with me to the grand jury as my lawyer. He would have to wait here, in this small conference room, for me to return after my testimony was over, or to meet with me privately if I should need a break during my grand jury testimony to confer with him.

When Zelinsky, Rhee, and Goldstein joined us in the small conference room, I was shocked to see that Rhee was wearing what appeared to be an expensive, possibly designer-made see-through blouse. Maybe my seventy-two years were showing but I had never imagined any woman would appear before a grand jury exposing her breasts to public view through a see-through blouse. I decided to refrain from a detailed observation or analysis of her obviously visible anatomy, deciding instead to concentrate on maintaining eye-contact when addressing her that morning.

Zelinsky began the questioning by asking me if I recalled while I was vacationing with my wife and family in Italy telling Roger Stone that Assange yet had Podesta emails that he planned to make public in October. I acknowledged that I knew in advance that Assange had Podesta's emails and that I did tell this to Roger Stone in August 2016, while I was still in Italy.

Next, Zelinsky focused on the email Roger Stone sent me on August 30, 2016, asking me to call him. As we discussed earlier, that led me to write a "cover-up memo" for him on John Podesta, suggesting that Roger's infamous Twitter post about "Podesta's time in the barrel" was a reference to my research about John and Tony Podesta's money dealings with Russia. Roger wanted to disguise his tweet, suggesting "Podesta's time in the barrel" was not a reference to any advanced knowledge Stone may have had from me, when I began telling Stone from Italy in emails dated earlier in August 2016 that I believed Assange had Podesta emails.

"We've examined your computer, Doctor Corsi," Zelinsky grilled me. "And we know that the next day, August 31, 2016, your birthday, you began at 7:30 a.m. to write that memo for Stone."

Before returning to Washington to appear before the grand jury, I had taken the time to research the file of my 2016 writing drafts that I had restored to my laptop from the Time Machine. I found that the file that I labeled, "ROGER STONE background PODESTA version 1.0 Aug. 31, 2016" was time-stamped for 12:17 p.m. that day. But I decided not to quibble with Zelinsky, so I agreed.

"Then, Doctor Corsi, we find from your computer that the first thing you did was to find a series of open source articles on Podesta and Russia that you could use in writing your memo for Roger Stone," Zelinsky said, pressing forward. "Is that correct?"

I vaguely remembered doing this, so once again I agreed.

Truthfully, I was astounded because it seemed as if the FBI had studied me down to knowing the key strokes that I had used on my computer to do Google searches for articles. I realized my Google file would have much information about my locations and my internet searches, but the way Zelinsky drilled down on how I wrote this article was shocking.

Repeatedly Zelinsky had warned me that I had no idea how truly extensive the Special Counselor's investigation had been. Now, I imagined an army of FBI computer specialists at Quantico mapping out my every electronic communication in 2016, including my emails, my cellphone calls, and my use of the laptop and the internet to conduct my research and write my various articles and memos.

"Yes, I recall that I wanted to find additional material to structure the article, other than the piece in the *Wall Street Journal* that Peter Schweizer published on July 31, 2016, and the report 'From Russia with Money' that his Government Accountability Institute published the next day," I answered.

"Why did you write the article in this manner?" Zelinsky asked.

"Because I wanted to create the impression that I had been researching Podesta and Russia for a long time," I continued.

"But, in fact, you had not been researching Podesta and Russia for a long time," Zelinsky said, continuing to drill down. "Isn't that true?"

"Correct," I answered. "I had read Schweizer's pieces earlier in the week and I was surprised to realize how much documentation there was in previously published open source material about the millions of dollars Podesta and Hillary were paid for sharing military technology, including the hypersonic missile technology Russia has used to make a nuclear weapon that cannot be shot down by U.S. missile defense."

"So, you knew this was a lie when you wrote the Podesta email?" Zelinsky asked, moving in for the kill on this line of questioning.

"Yes, I did," I admitted. "In politics, it's not unusual to create alternative explanations to deflect the attacks of your political opponents."

Besides, the memo had a strong element of truth in that Podesta had gotten up to $35 million investment from the Russians plus stock through a shell corporation Russia had established in the Netherlands for money laundering all as an apparent pay-off for selling to Russia the U.S. military technology under the ruse of Hillary's "reset" policy as secretary of state.

But Zelinsky was completely uninterested in learning more about the possible crimes Hillary and Podesta may have committed, for millions of dollars in return. All Zelinsky wanted to know was that I wrote that memo to provide Stone with an alternative explanation for his "Podesta's time in the barrel" tweet.

Public relations work is not specifically considered lying. It was considered completely appropriate when British Petroleum, a company that had been exploiting petroleum resources worldwide for decades at the behest of the British government, changed its name to "BP," with the slogan "Beyond Petroleum."

I had worked my way through college by working, following my father's career by working for public relations. My father arranged for me to be hired by Edward Howard & Co., a public relations firm in Cleveland, Ohio. There I had worked on Republican Seth Taft's mayoral campaign against Carl Stokes, who in 1967 first African American elected mayor of a major U.S. city. At that time, I was an undergraduate, finishing my last year of college at Case Western Reserve University.

I still do not consider what I wrote for Stone to have been immoral or illegal. Zelinsky was the one not playing fair by granting Hillary the right to use public relations to cover up any number of possible crimes. But when it came to me and Roger Stone, we were criminals for having engaged in the type of public relations positioning that is standard operating procedures for political campaigns in the United States today.

Next, Zelinsky began asking whether I was aware that Stone had used my Podesta memo as the basis for his testimony under oath before the House Intelligence Committee on September 26, 2017.

Here, David Gray asked for a break, so he could confer with the prosecutors. After a few minutes, David returned and informed me that Rhee, Zelinsky, and Goldstein had agreed to give me a grant of immunity for my testimony here. David explained to me that I could be criminally charged for subornation of perjury for my role in creating a "cover story" about Podesta that Stone used in his testimony under oath to the House Intelligence Committee.

We proceeded to execute the verbal agreement, with Zelinsky assuring us the written agreement would arrive for our signatures in a few minutes. The agreement for "limited use immunity" arrived shortly and was signed by all after being read. David had explained to me that the grant of immunity extended only to protect me in that my testimony to the grand jury on the House Intelligence Committee could not be used to prosecute me for the crime of subornation of perjury.

When he was finished getting down my testimony on the various Podesta cover-up documents I had written for Stone, Zelinsky shifted to drilling down on the coincidence of Assange holding the release of the Podesta file until after the *Washington Post* reported the Billy Bush tape on October 7, 2016.

"Did Roger Stone tell you in advance that the Billy Bush tape was going to be released?" Zelinsky asked me.

"Yes, he did," I admitted. Although I could not remember exactly when Roger told me, or the precise substance of the discussion, I remembered Roger told me before the *Washington Post* went to press with the Billy Bush tape that the tape was coming and that it would be a bombshell. I recall that I knew in advance that Donald Trump could be heard on the tape bragging about grabbing women by their genitals.

"And was Mister Stone disturbed about the release of the Billy Bush tape?" Zelinsky asked.

"Yes," I answered. Stone's strategy to have Trump win involved gaining a larger than expected percentage of women voters. Obviously, Trump's comments on the tape would be especially offensive to women.

"What did Mister Stone want you to do to blunt the impact of the Billy Bush tape?" Zelinsky asked.

"He wanted me to see if I could get Assange to begin dropping the Podesta emails on top of the *Washington Post* exposé," I admitted. Obviously, Stone wanted Assange to begin dropping the Podesta emails because Stone knew the explosive content that we expected the Podesta emails to contain would compete with the Billy Bush tape for the news cycle. This would blunt the negative impact on the Trump campaign of the Billy Bush revelations.

"What did you do in response to Mister Stone's request?" Zelinsky asked, moving in for the kill a second time.

"I do not recall that I had any source in contact with Assange that I could instruct," I told Zelinsky.

I continued: "But I believe I may have posted some tweets and I believe I told the daily World Net Daily news team conference call that the Billy Bush tape was coming. I'm sure I asked that if anybody had a way to reach Assange, we should pass the alert to Assange, so he could begin dropping the Podesta file right away."

Having gotten the answers he wanted, after drilling me in rapid-fire fashion, Zelinsky announced we were ready to go to the grand jury.

Entering the grand jury for the first time was another frightening experience. I had never before testified to a grand jury and I knew David Gray would not be permitted to accompany me.

The grand jury room was about the size of an average university graduate school classroom. It was tiered with the grand jury members sitting in rows that reached from the front of the classroom to the back wall. As I entered the room and scanned the grand jury members, it was immediately obvious that the grand jury was made up of Washington middle class residents, consisting predominately of minorities. The back row against the wall consisted entirely of African American males who looked angry.

My guess was that I was guilty from the start with these grand jury members. If any of them knew my past writings—and I guessed the Special Counsel had briefed the grand jury on me and my background in preparation for my testimony—I guessed these people hated my politics and considered me a "conspiracy theory" liar, maybe even a member of some "white supremacy hate group." After all, I had served as Washington Bureau Chief for Alex Jones and Infowars.com, an arch-enemy of the hard left.

In the front of the grand jury room, I was shown a seat behind a long table. To my immediate right sat the stenographer, ready to make a word-for-word transcript of my testimony. To my left, Rhee and Goldstein sat. At my far left, Zelinsky stood at a podium. It was clear that Zelinsky would lead the questioning. From time to time,

Rhee and Goldstein would whisper to one another, after which they passed a written note to Zelinsky.

The foreman of the grand jury asked me to rise and I took an oath to "tell the truth, the whole truth, and nothing but the truth, so help me God."

Zelinsky's questions were all precisely phrased. In a courtroom, the questions might have been considered leading questions.

"Doctor Corsi, did Mister Stone telephone you on the evening of August 30, 2016?" My answer was yes.

Each question telegraphed the answer that Zelinsky expected, with the questions mimicking the questions Zelinsky had asked me in the small conference room that morning. When the questioning began, I maintained eye-contact with Zelinsky, taking pains not to look at the grand jury members at all. I knew what was critical here was the record the stenographer was taking. That was the record that would be used should a prosecutor want to indict me for lying to the grand jury. How the grand jury voted was inconsequential to me, since I was appearing as a witness, not as a target of the grand jury investigation.

The testimony took about thirty minutes in total. I admitted to working with Stone to develop the Podesta cover-up story and I admitted Stone had asked me on October 7, 2016, to get Assange to start dropping the Podesta emails immediately, so as to compete in the news cycle with the Billy Bush exposé. The vast majority of my answers to the grand jury were one-word "yes" or "no," in response to Zelinsky's questions. All I had to do to get through the grand jury was to follow Zelinsky's lead.

I was relieved to be excused from the grand jury, my testimony complete. I joined David Gray back in the small conference room for a few minutes before Zelinsky asked to speak with David privately.

When David returned to the small conference room, he gave me a "thumbs up" signal, holding his hand very close to his chest so only I could see the gesture.

To my surprise, Zelinsky, Rhee, and Goldstein, followed by the FBI agents who had been present, followed David into the small conference room. Each of them shook my hand and congratulated me.

Zelinsky was especially pleased.

"Not bad for an Ignatius man," he said. In our initial conversations, getting to know one another before first day's questioning started, Zelinsky also noted that I had graduated from St. Ignatius High School, a well-known Jesuit school in Cleveland, Ohio. Although I graduated Ignatius in 1968 and Zelinsky was much younger, I recalled he said his wife had an association with Gilmore Academy, a private, Catholic, coed school located in Gates Mills, Ohio. Even in my era, girls from Gilmore Academy frequently dated the guys from Ignatius.

Being driven back to the Mayflower from the FBI, I felt relieved. I hoped my ordeal with the Special Prosecutor was over now that my grand jury appearance was done. Despite many lapses of memory and repeated threats from the prosecutors that I had already said enough to be charged with lying to the FBI, I believed the celebratory handshakes at the end of my testimony meant all was forgiven. Why would Mueller charge me with lying to the FBI if the Special Counselor's office planned on using my testimony to indict Roger Stone, I wondered? Clearly, undermining my credibility by charging me with perjury would be the last thing Mueller would want to do if Zelinsky, Rhee, and Goldstein felt my testimony was critical to indicting and convicting Stone.

As I evaluated my own testimony, I felt the only crime I might have committed was not objecting to Stone using my Podesta memo in his sworn testimony before the House Intel Committee. But, in reality, all I had admitted that what Stone or I had committed was the "crime" of practicing politics, or more precisely the "crime" of having supported Donald Trump for the presidency against Hillary Clinton in 2016. If everyone who lied in a political campaign had been criminally prosecuted for the crime of not telling the truth, every politician and political operative would be arrested, tried, and put in prison. When it came to the House Intel Committee, witnesses are allowed to alter their testimony when inconvenient facts "prove" they had lied in their initial sworn testimony.

Why it was so important to Mueller to prove Stone had advance knowledge in August 2016 that Assange had Podesta's emails was a mystery to me.

Under various Supreme Court rulings, I was allowed to contact Assange, to meet with him, and to interview him, even if Assange was in receipt of stolen DNC emails. As a political operative, I could not see that Stone had committed any crime by wanting to know what additional material adverse to Hillary Clinton that Assange may have had after the drop of DNC emails on July 22, 2016, just before the start of the Democrat's nominating convention in Philadelphia.

At dinner, David Gray burst the bubble. While he felt I had done perfect in my grand jury testimony, he said Zelinsky told him the Special Counsel's office might want to call me back to question me more about who my source to Assange was. I was devastated to think this was only round one and that I would be called back for yet another grand jury appearance.

But this time, I feared Zelinsky, Rhee, and Goldstein would not be so forgiving.

CHAPTER 9

Assange, Russia, and Hillary

Sunday, November 18, 2018

Last night, I was plagued by nightmares that caused me to sleep very poorly. I am feeling chest pains intensifying and the tightness is making it difficult to breathe. My fear that I will suffer a stroke, or maybe a heart attack is growing daily. Right now, I am planning to see if I can schedule with my cardiologist an emergency visit tomorrow. But I am going to continue writing. I am determined to tell the truth of my horror-show inquisition at the hands of the politically motivated Mueller Special Counsel investigation, even if it kills me.

Please understand that I have never met, spoken with, or otherwise communicated with Julian Assange, except to post tweets that included @JulianAssange or #WikiLeaks. I never had a source who was in contact with Assange—a source that could provide me with accurate information about what Assange was planning to do.

Yes, I would have been pleased if Ted Malloch went to see Assange in London—I realized this the moment I finally saw my 2016 emails, after the first disastrous interview with Mueller's henchmen. Reviewing my emails, I also realized I would have gone to London to contact Assange if Joseph Farah, for whom I worked as a reporter at WND.com for some twelve years, had bought me an airline ticket and assigned me to travel to London to meet Assange as part of my job as a full-time staff reporter. But I never believed Malloch would follow through with Roger Stone's request to "Get Assange," and I doubted Joseph Farah had the free cash to send me to London on this assignment.

I am going to write this chapter to explain to you, the reader, how I used my basic intuitive skills as a reporter to figure out in August 2016 that Assange had Podesta's emails, that Assange planned to start making the Podesta file public in October 2016, and that Assange would release the emails in a serial, day-by-day fashion, right up to election day.

I am also going to explain why I believe the "Russia Collusion" story was fabricated by Hillary Clinton and John Podesta after the DNC realized in March 2016 Podesta's emails had been breached. I am going to conclude by explaining why I believe Mueller's Special Counsel investigation was a Deep State plan to continue the cover-up of a yet on-going coup d'état against Donald Trump planned by Barack Obama, Hillary Clinton, and the traitorous Deep State operatives that still today control the U.S. intelligence agencies, including both the CIA and the National Security Agency, as well as the Department of Justice and the FBI.

My understanding of Assange began in February 2016 when a source I will name "LH" to preserve here anonymity started emailing me the first of what would become dozens of emails explaining to me in detail how the Democrats put together their computer systems. At first, I was skeptical, but after I began verifying LH's information, I finally realized her information was authentic and reliable.

I ultimately figured out LH's identity and I telephoned her ex-husband, who turned out to be a retired, relatively high-ranking official of the National Security Agency. LH's husband was startled by my call, but he explained to me that he felt his former wife had serious psychological problems. I was pleased to have identified LH, but her ex-husband's concern failed to dissuade me that LH was giving me invaluable insight into how the Democrats had created their computer systems for presidential elections. LH knew what she was talking about, dating back to Zack Exley, a little-known but very important hard left political operative who rose to prominence within leftist political circles in 2004, when John Kerry was running for president.

The DNC computer mafia had roots in Colorado, where many of them went to school together. This cadre of computer whiz kids worked in Obama's campaign before they created Hillary's private email server when she was secretary of state. With Soros funding ties providing much of the needed cash, this DNC computer mafia moved into both Hillary Clinton's presidential campaign and into the DNC under Debbie Wasserman Schultz. In 2016 through early 2018, I reported extensively in WND.com and Infowars.com about how this Colorado computer mafia operated.

The key insight you must understand is that these Democratic computer whiz kids created different computer systems for different purposes. Hillary's private email server had nothing to do with the DNC computer systems. The main DNC computer system was used by candidates, known as NGP-VAN. The NGP-VAN system contained the DNC's voter data—data shared in common by Hillary Clinton and Bernie Sanders—as well as donor lists and opposition research that was held separately by the Clinton and Sanders campaign. The NGP-VAN system did not archive emails of John Podesta or of the other officials in Hillary's campaign or in the DNC.

While Hillary's campaign and the DNC were two separate organizations, Hillary's campaign used the DNC's NGP-VAN system (as did Bernie Sanders) to run their campaign fund-raising and get-out-the-vote activities. The NGP-VAN system was designed with a firewall such that Hillary's campaign and Sanders' campaign could each access the DNC voter and donor databases maintained in common by the DNC for all Democratic Party presidential campaigns. The firewall was supposed to prevent the Clinton campaign and the Sanders campaign from seeing the analytic work done for each campaign after each campaign drew on the voter and donor database the DNC held in common.

Finally, neither Hillary's private email server nor the NGP-VAN system had anything to do with the email server residing within the DNC where the emails of John Podesta, as well as other campaign and DNC officials, were archived.

The main point you have to understand is that investigative research techniques, used commonly by law enforcement detectives, by intelligence analysts, and by press reporters like me proceeds by first identifying what computer data was stolen and secondly by determining which computer system archived that data. Proceeding this way, it becomes obvious the Democrats suffered multiple different computer attacks and the emails Assange had could only have come from the DNC email server, not from Hillary's private email server or from the NGP-VAN system.

Next, let me explain a few important timeline points.

On March 16, 2016, WikiLeaks published a searchable archive of 30,322 emails and email attachments that came from Hillary Clinton's private email server when she was secretary of state. All of these thirty-thousand emails had been previously published. All of the 30,322 emails had been previously published by other sources and were generally obtained as a result of Freedom of Information Act [FOIA] requests. The only unique thing WikiLeaks published was a "portal" that permitted these 30,322 previously available Hillary Clinton emails to be searched.

On June 12, 2016, the *Guardian* in London reported that Assange said WikiLeaks was preparing to publish more emails that Hillary Clinton sent and received while secretary of state.[34] Assange did not specify whether these Clinton emails came from her private email server or not. At this time, I suspected Assange might have obtained

---

34   Tran, Mark. "WikiLeaks to publish more Hillary Clinton emails—
       Julian Assange," *The Guardian*, June 12, 2016. *https://www.theguardian.com/
       media/2016/jun/12/wikileaks-to-publish-more-hillary-clinton-emails-
       julian-assange.*

more Hillary Clinton emails hacked by an external source or stolen by an internal source from her private email server. This never materialized to be the case. Assange never published for the first time any emails from Hillary's private email server.

On Sunday, June 12, 2016, Assange gave a television interview to Robert Peston on the British commercial network, ITV.[35] In that interview, Assange disclosed that WikiLeaks has "upcoming leaks in relation to Hillary Clinton," though Assange distinguished the Hillary Clinton emails WikiLeaks possessed pending publication came from a different source than the emails from Hillary's private email server. This alerted me to the possibility Assange had obtained emails from the DNC email server.

Then, on June 14, 2016, the *Washington Post* reported that unnamed Russian government hackers penetrated the computer system of the DNC and gained access to the entire database of opposition research on GOP presidential candidate Donald Trump.[36] The *Washington Post* noted that the hackers had access to the DNC network for about a year but were expelled in June "in a major computer cleanup campaign." The newspaper also reported that no financial or donor information was stolen. I immediately concluded that this hack involved the NGP-VAN system that included opposition research, donor information, and voter information. The *Washington Post* said nothing about emails from Clinton campaign or DNC officials having been hacked as well.

---

35   "Assange on Peston on Sunday: 'More Clinton leaks to come,'" ITV News, June 12, 2016. *https://www.itv.com/news/update/2016-06-12/assange-on-peston-on-sunday-more-clinton-leaks-to-come/*.

36   Nakashima, Ellen. "Russian government hackers penetrated DNC, stole opposition research on Trump," *Washington Post*, June 14, 2016. *https://www.washingtonpost.com/world/national-security/russian-government-hackers-penetrated-dnc-stole-opposition-research-on-trump/2016/06/14/cf006cb4-316e-11e6-8ff7-7b6c1998b7a0_story.html?utm_term=.8aefbe5deb85*.

When I searched the *Washington Post* article to find out how the DNC was responsible for this hack, I realized the newspaper was quoting Michael Sussman, a lawyer from Perkins Coie who was cited as a DNC lawyer. I knew Perkins Coie because that was the law firm that played an intimate insider role for Barack Obama in the cover-up surrounding Obama's birth certificate.

The article also identified that the technical examination of the DNC computer hack had been undertaken by CrowdStrike Services Inc., a cybersecurity firm that had been funded to the tune of a hundred million dollars in 2016 by Google Capital, then an arm of Alphabet Inc., Google's parent company.[37] In 2016, Eric Schmidt, the chairman of Alphabet, was working inside Hillary Clinton's campaign to organize for her the campaign's computer-driven get-out-the-vote (GOTV) effort. Interestingly, the DNC evidently failed to disclose to the *Washington Post* that the particular system that had been hacked was the NGP-VAN system, not Hillary's private email server and not the DNC's email server.

The *Washington Post* also reported that DNC leaders knew of the hack as early as April 2016, when DNC chief executive Amy Dacey got a phone call from her operations chief alerting her that the DNC information technology team had noticed unusual network activity on the DNC computer systems. If the DNC knew in April that the computer breach had occurred, why did the DNC wait until June to make that fact known? I began to conclude the DNC, with the assistance of Perkins Coie, Eric Schmidt, and CrowdStrike had manufactured evidence that would pin the breach on Russia.

On June 15, 2016, one day after the *Washington Post* report on the breach of the NGP-VAN system at the DNC, Dmitri Alperovitch, the co-founder and chief technology officer for CrowdStrike, published an article insisting that CrowdStrike stood by its analysis

---

37   Klein, Aaron. "DNC 'Russian Hacking' Conclusion Comes from
      Google-Linked Firm," Breitbart.com, January 6, 2017.

and findings that two separate Russian intelligence-affiliated adversaries had penetrated the DNC computer network in May 2016.[38] Alperovitch indicated that CrowdStrike had identified two sophisticated computer adversaries on the DNC network—COZY BEAR and FANCY BEAR—both identified as trademarks of Russia-based cyberattack intelligence groups that U.S. intelligence operatives have recognized since 2000 as Russian-based cyber-espionage intelligence groups with close ties to the Russian government's "powerful and highly capable intelligence services."

The Alperovitch article was written in response to a blog post to a WordPress site "authored by an individual using the moniker Guccifer 2.0" who claimed credit for breaching the DNC.[39] "Worldwide known cyber security company CrowdStrike announced that the Democratic National Committee (DNC) servers had been hacked by 'sophisticated' hacker groups," Guccifer 2.0 wrote under the heading "DNC's Servers Hacked by Lone Hacker." Guccifer 2.0 bragged that hacking the DNC's servers was "easy, very easy." "Guccifer (the first Guccifer 1.0 Marcel Lazar) may have been the first one who penetrated Hillary Clinton's and other Democrats' mail servers," Guccifer 2.0 noted. "But he certainly wasn't the last. No wonder any other hacker could easily get access to the DNC's servers." Then Guccifer 2.0 bragged: "Shame on CrowdStrike: Do you think I've been in the DNC's networks for almost a year and saved only two documents? Do you really believe it? Here are just a few docs from the many thousands I extracted when hacking into the DNC's networks."

---

38 Alperovitch, Dmitri. "Bears in the Midst: Intrusion into the Democratic National Committee," CrowdStrike Blog, June 15, 2016. *https://www.crowdstrike.com/blog/bears-midst-intrusion-democratic-national-committee/*.

39 Guccifer 2.0, "Guccifer 2.0 DNC's Servers Hacked by a Lone Hacker," WordPress.com, June 15, 2016. *https://guccifer2.wordpress.com/2016/06/15/dnc/*.

Over the next few weeks, Guccifer 2.0 published a trove of documents in various publications, including on his own blog. I downloaded all of these documents and studied them. Guccifer 2.0 hacked opposition research on Trump, various voter and donor analyses that appeared to have come from the Clinton campaigns, plus numerous DNC internal memorandums. But what was missing in the Guccifer 2.0 publication of DNC hacked documents were emails, suggesting Guccifer 2.0 had not penetrated the DNC email server, or the private email archives of John Podesta and other Clinton campaign officials.

The Guccifer 2.0 controversy flared again when the *Wall Street Journal* published on May 25, 2017, published an article claiming Guccifer 2.0 had sent Aaron Nevins, a GOP Republican consultant in Florida, 2.5 gigabytes of Democratic Congressional Campaign Committee (housed in the same building with the DNC) documents, some of which Nevins published on a blog HelloFLA.com that Nevins ran using a pseudonym.[40] Nevins told the Wall Street Journal he set up a Dropbox account "so whoever was using the Guccifer 2.0 name could send large amounts of material." The purpose of this article was to connect Roger Stone to Guccifer 2.0, in an attempt to buttress the Hillary-Podesta "Russian Collusion" narrative.

This episode confirms that Guccifer 2.0 had hacked only the DNC computers, the donor and voter data, plus various opposition research analyses, and various DNC memorandum—all from the NPG-VAN computer servers that the DNC maintained in Massachusetts and in Washington. Guccifer 2.0 confirmed this in a post to his WordPress site posted on January 12, 2017, in which Guccifer 2.0 wrote the following: "I already explained at The Future of Cyber Security Europe conference that took place in London in last September, I

---

40   Berzon, Alexandra and Barry, Rob. "How Alleged Russian Hacker Teamed up with Florida GOP Operative," *Wall Street Journal,* May 27, 2017. *https://www.wsj.com/articles/how-alleged-russian-hacker-teamed-up-with-florida-gop-operative-1495724787.*

had used a different way to breach into the DNC network. I found a vulnerability in the NGP-VAN software installed in the DNC system."[41] Guccifer 2.0 never bragged that he hacked the DNC email server that contained the Podesta emails.

It is important to understand Assange never published any information involving donor lists or voter analysis, not of the type that Guccifer 2.0 published on websites such as "DCLeaks." As I plan to demonstrate in this chapter, the WikiLeaks drops of DNC emails on July 22, 2016 and on October 7, 2016 came from the DNC email server—a completely different computer system in the DNC that Guccifer 2.0 never appears to have accessed.

Guccifer 1.0, the Romanian Marcel Lazar, was arrested in Romania on January 22, 2014 and convicted to four years in prison, where he remained until he was extradited to the United States in March 2016. On September 1, 2016, a U.S. district judge in Alexandria, Virginia, sentenced Guccifer 1.0 to four years in federal prison, after he pleaded guilty to one count each of aggravated identity theft and unauthorized access to a protected computer.

In contrast, Guccifer 2.0 has never been positively identified, let alone arrested.

Yet, the much-touted U.S. intelligence estimate continues to blame Guccifer 2.0 as the hacker involved in stealing the Podesta emails and giving them to WikiLeaks. On January 6, 2017, the office of the Director of National Intelligence released a report entitled, "Background to 'Assessing Russian Activities and Intentions in Recent U.S. Elections': The Analytic Process and Cyber Incident Attribution." This report concluded "with high confidence" that Russian military intelligence "used the Guccifer 2.0 persona" to release the Podesta files to WikiLeaks, but the report also admitted the identification of the origin of a cybersecurity attack was "difficult"

41   Guccifer 2.0, "Here I Am Again, My Friends!" WordPress.com, January 12, 2017, *https://guccifer2.wordpress.com/2017/01/12/fake-evidence/*.

based only on "tradecraft" that relies on circumstantial evidence at best, presuming a hacker leaves a signature, such that cyberattacks like "Cozy Bear" and "Fancy Bear" can be reliably be attributed to Russian intelligence operatives.

The attribution of "Cozy Bear" and "Fancy Bear" to Russia was further undermined by the WikiLeaks release of stolen CIA internal documents that described in excruciating detail the extensive capabilities the CIA has developed to launch cyberattacks—an ability that extends to planting metadata so that cybersecurity firms will attribute the hack to Russia, when the real culprit was the CIA.

On March 7, 2017, WikiLeaks released 8,761 documents on the CIA's "global covert hacking program" that included documents from a project called "Umbrage" proving the CIA could launch "false flag" cyberattacks and make them look as if they originated from other countries, such as Russia. "The CIA's Remote Devices Branch's UMBRAGE group collects and maintains a substantial library of attack techniques 'stolen' from malware produced in other states including the Russian Federation," WikiLeaks noted. "With UMBRAGE and related projects the CIA cannot only increase its total number of attack types but also misdirect attribution by leaving behind the 'fingerprints' of the groups that the attack techniques were stolen from," WikiLeaks continued.

Now, I know this is tedious and will tax many readers, so I've decided here to take a break. You have to understand what I am going through is a roller-coaster. Sometimes I feel like everything is normal and that the federal government will understand that I am a reporter and should be protected by the First Amendment. Then, I realize that the next ring of the doorbell could be the FBI seeking to handcuff me and arrest me in full view of my family. I have gone public saying that I expect to be indicted any day now by the FBI for lying to the FBI—a charge I consider preposterous given the extents to which I went to cooperate with Mueller's investigation.

Besides, the chest pains are returning, and I need to rest for a while.

Ↄ Ↄ Ↄ

Resuming after a much-needed break, we need only a few more dates to complete the analysis.

On July 22, 2016, Wikileaks began releasing over two days a total of 44,053 emails and 17,761 email attachments from key figures in the DNC. What I noticed immediately was that the largest number of emails by far came from DNC Communications Director Luis Miranda (10,520 emails), who had approximately three times the emails released for the next highest on the list, National Finance Director Jordon Kaplan (3,799 emails) and Finance Chief of Staff Scott Corner (3,095 emails). What I noticed immediately was that emails from Debbie Wasserman Schultz and John Podesta were missing. Yet, by analyzing the addresses in the emails, it was clear the "From," "To," and or "CC" listings indicate the email was sent by or to an addressee using the DNC email server, identified as @dnc.org.

From this analysis, I immediately concluded that Assange had obtained these emails from the DNC email server, not from Hillary Clinton's private email server, or from the NGP-VAN servers. Obviously, Debbie Wasserman Schultz was the target of this email dump, given that the main import of the emails was to reveal the scheming done by Debbie Wasserman Schultz and the Clinton campaign to steal the nomination from Bernie Sanders by manipulating the primaries. While the DNC email server could have been hacked by an outside agent, what is equally plausible is that the emails could have been stolen by someone on the inside of the DNC, perhaps an employee with their own @dnc.org email address.

If obtaining the DNC emails was an "inside job," downloading the emails would have been as simple as accessing each official's email account and downloading all emails listed there. The WikiLeaks emails released the Friday before the Monday, July 25, 2016, start of the Democratic National Convention had the immediate impact of forcing DNC Chair Debbie Wasserman Schultz to resign under fire on Sunday, July 24—a move that threw the national nominating convention into disarray. Clearly, I reasoned there had to have been Podesta emails on that server that would have discussed the Clinton/DNC plot to deny Bernie Sanders the Democratic Party presidential nomination in 2016. Where were these Podesta emails, I wondered?

Then, on July 26, 2016, Assange gave an interview to CNN in which he claimed he had "a lot more material," in addition to the 44,053 DNC emails that Assange had dropped on July 22, 2016.[42] Assange added that the Clinton campaign's rush to blame Russia raised "serious questions…about the natural instincts of Clinton that when confronted with a serious domestic political scandal, she tries to blame the Russians, blame the Chinese, et cetera."[43] In the interview, Assange distinguished his drop of DNC emails from other previous hacks—a discussion that I took to confirm Assange's DNC emails came from the DNC email server, the only server with the address @dnc.com. Listening to this interview on CNN, all the pieces fit in place for me. Assange had Podesta emails that were also lifted from the DNC server and these were the emails he was holding to drop later in the campaign.

Determined to study John Podesta, I have made it a point over the years to attend public meetings in Washington that he chaired. I recognized Podesta as a highly intelligent and very experienced Washington insider, who over decades has moved to the ascendancy

---

42   Chance, Matthew. "Julian Assange: 'A lot more material' coming
      on US elections," CNN Politics, July 27, 2017. *https://www.cnn.
      com/2016/07/26/politics/julian-assange-dnc-email-leak-hack/.*

43   Kirby, Jen. "Assange Says WikiLeaks Might Release More Documents
      Relating to 2016 Race," *New York Magazine*, July 27, 2016. *http://
      nymag.com/intelligencer/2016/07/wikileaks-might-publish-more-docs-on-
      election.html.*

of leftist public policy development. While Podesta was Hillary's campaign chairman, I was certain Podesta and Hillary's personalities would clash, that Podesta would worry about Hillary's temper and her health. Podesta for a while chaired the Clinton Foundation—a fact few remember—and he had to know from the inside that the Clinton Foundation was a criminal fraud, not a charity, but instead a massive international crime syndicate that specialized in laundering third world money.

I felt certain that if Assange had Podesta's emails he would wait to drop them in October 2016, capturing the chance to stage the 2016 "October Surprise," a term that had been in vogue in U.S. presidential politics since 1980 when Jimmy Carter lost re-election to Ronald Reagan, largely because the Reagan camp finessed Ayatollah Khomeini to postpone the release of the hostages from the American embassy in Tehran until after that year's November election. I also figured that Assange would release the Podesta emails in drip-by-drip fashion, serially, over a number of days, stretching right up to the Election Day. In presidential politics, the news cycle speeds up, such that what might take a month or a week to play out in a normal news cycle might take only a day or two in the heightened intensity of a presidential news cycle—especially a presidential news cycle in October, right at Election Day is nearing.

I have also studied Assange over the years, although always from a distance. What I know is that Assange releases his material strategically. Clearly, Assange knew that by releasing the DNC emails on July 22, 2016, as Democratic delegates were traveling to Philadelphia to attend the convention, there would be no time for the Democrats to manage the news cycle. By dropping over forty-thousand DNC emails over two days, Assange dominated the news cycle, forcing Debbie Wasserman Schultz to resign on the Saturday before the convention gavel fell to start the proceedings.

An October drop was different. In college, attending a class on English literature, I realized Charles Dickens novels were so long, in large part, because he published them serially, as daily new chapters in the penny newspaper tabloids sold in London at the time. While it is commonly said that Dickens was "paid by the word," it is much less appreciated that Dickens planned his novels to be lengthy, so he could serialize them in the London newspapers. Dickens knew that London readers would discuss each day's chapter in the coffee houses and salons of the time, building anticipation for what would come next.

Assange understands the same principle of serialization.

Starting October 7, 2018, Assange dropped 57,153 emails in the Podesta file over in thirty-four parts, releasing one and sometimes two parts per day, with the last drop occurring three days after the election on November 8, 2016. The key point to me was the realization that Assange thinks strategically. When the drop gets maximum impact by dropping all the material at once, as was the case with in July 22, 2016, when the goal was to knock out Debbie Wasserman Schultz and to drive Hillary's coronation nominating convention into chaos, Assange dropped the material all at once, just before the convention in Philadelphia was about to begin. With the Podesta emails, the October-drop strategy called for serialization. It really is pretty obvious when you think about it.

The last piece of the puzzle fell in place for me when Seth Rich, an IT worker in the DNC was murdered on July 10, 2016, at approximately 4:30 a.m. EST, as he walked home along the streets of Washington, D.C. The Washington Police Department has kept the investigation of Seth Rich's murder secret, refusing to release basic information such as an autopsy, or conclusions from police investigative reports. The murder was initially reported as a "robbery gone bad," until it was realized that Seth Rich still had his wallet, a $2,000 gold necklace, and his wrist watch on him when he was shot. Police rushed to the scene as neighbors heard two gunshots being fired. The assailant(s) fled the scene before police arrived. No assailant has ever been charged with the murder.

The strongest indication that Seth Rich leaked the DNC and Podesta emails to WikiLeaks comes from Julian Assange himself.

In an interview broadcast on the Dutch television program Nieuwswuur on August 9, 2016, the host Eelco Bosch van Rosenthal asked Assange, "The stuff that you're sitting on, is an October Surprise in there?"

Assange insisted, "WikiLeaks never sits on material," even though Assange had previously said WikiLeaks yet has more material related to the Hillary Clinton campaign that had yet to be published.

Then, on his own initiative, without being specifically asked, Assange began talking about Seth Rich.

"Whistleblowers go to significant efforts to get us material, and often very significant risks," Assange volunteered.

"There's a twenty-seven-year-old that works for the DNC who was shot in the back, murdered, just a few weeks ago, for unknown reasons, as he was walking down the streets in Washington," Assange continued.

Van Rosenthal objected that the murder of DNC staffer Seth Rich was a robbery.

"No, there's no findings," Assange answered.

"What are you suggesting?" Van Rosenthal interjected.

"I'm suggesting that our sources take risks and they become concerned to see things occurring like that," Assange responded.

There was no reason for Assange to have spontaneously brought up Seth Rich in the context of the risks his leakers take if Rich were not the leaker involved in the DNC and Podesta emails that WikiLeaks published.

On August 9, 2016, WikiLeaks offered a $20,000 reward "for information leading to the conviction for the murder of DNC staffer Seth Rich."

Again, why would WikiLeaks do this if Seth Rich were not the leaker in question?

Assange has repeatedly denied that the Russians "or any state party" supplied WikiLeaks with the DNC and/or Podesta emails.[44]

Speaking plainly, Assange—a political operative with an established reputation of telling the truth—has denied the Russians or any state actor was involved, knowing he was leaving the clear impression the DNC and Podesta emails traced back to a leaker internal to the DNC—the same conclusion President Obama suggested in his final press conference.

More convincing evidence that the Russians were not involved in the WikiLeaks drops was published by the left-leaning nation in an article where former NSA experts concluded the Wikileaks drop of DNC emails resulted not from an outside hacking attack, but as the result of a leak, an inside job by someone who had access to the DNC computer system.[45] A memo prepared by the Veteran Intelligence Professionals for Sanity (VIPS) based on their own investigation, concluded that the theft of DNC emails was not a hack, but "some kind of inside leak that did not involve Russia."

VIPS asked President Obama to disclose any evidence that Wikileaks received DNC data from the Russians. VIPS noted that President Obama at a press conference on January 18, 2017, described the conclusions of the intelligence community as "not conclusive," even though the Intelligence Community Assessment of January 6, 2017 had expressed "high confidence" that Russian intelligence had relayed material it acquired from the DNC to Wikileaks.

---

44   Ye Hee Lee, Michael. "Julian Assange's claim that there was no Russian involvement in WikiLeaks emails," *Washington Post*, January 5, 2017. *https://www.washingtonpost.com/news/fact-checker/wp/2017/01/05/julian-assanges-claim-that-there-was-no-russian-involvement-in-wikileaks-emails/?utm_term=.ab964aa1f425.*

45   Lawrence, Patrick. "A New Report Raises Big Questions About Last Year's DNC Hack," The Nation, August 9, 2017, *https://www.thenation.com/article/a-new-report-raises-big-questions-about-last-years-dnc-hack/.*

"Obama's admission came as no surprise to us," the VIPS report concluded. "It has long been clear to us that the reason the U.S. government lacks conclusive evidence of a transfer of a 'Russian hack' to WikiLeaks is because there was no such transfer. Based mostly on the cumulatively unique technical experience of our ex-NSA colleagues, we have been saying for almost a year that the DNC data reached WikiLeaks via a copy/leak by a DNC insider."

In the final analysis, what surprised me the most was that Mueller's prosecutors and the FBI questioning me were completely uninterested in my explaining why I believe I figured out on my own in August 2016 that Assange had Podesta's emails yet to drop. When I first decided to cooperate with Mueller, I felt the prosecutors would be interested in my analysis. I could not have been more wrong.

Jeannie Rhee dismissed as a "narrative" my explanation of how I connected the dots. The Special Prosecutor's office was locked into the conclusion that "the Russians did it," and they were uninterested in any answer that suggested the contrary.

After I was repeatedly accused of lying by a combination of Rhee, Zelinsky, and Goldstein, I resigned myself to the conclusion that the Special Prosecutor had a narrative and was only interested in testimony that affirmed their pre-determined narrative. That narrative was as simple as it was wrong.

Mueller and company had decided the Trump campaign somehow encouraged Russia to steal the DNC emails and give them to Assange, so WikiLeaks could publish them. Then to establish "Russian collusion" with the Trump campaign, Mueller was out to connect his own dots. The Mueller prosecutors had been charged with the mission to grill me until I would "give up" my source to Assange. I was their critical "missing link."

If Rhee, Zelinsky, and Goldstein only got me to confess, Mueller figured he could connect the dots from Roger Stone to me to Assange, and from Assange back again to me, and from me to Roger Stone, who would feed the information to Steve Bannon, then chairing the Trump campaign.

The final dots, the Mueller prosecutors assumed, would connect Bannon to Trump and the "Russian collusion" chain of communication would be complete.

The only problem was that I did not have a source connecting me to Assange, so Mueller's chain-link narrative does not connect.

When I could not provide the Special Counsel's office with the answers they wanted to hear, the three prosecutors, Rhee, Zelinsky, and Goldstein, blew up on cue, stormed out of the room, and threatened to put me in prison for the rest of my life—all despite the fact that I never once lied to them.

On November 15, 2018, President Trump tweeted four scathing, but accurate messages about the Mueller inquisition:

> *The inner workings of the Mueller investigation are a total mess. They have found no collusion and have gone absolutely nuts. They are screaming and shouting at people, horribly threatening them to come up with the answers they want. They are a disgrace to our Nation and don't...*

> *...care how many lives they ruin. These are Angry People, including the highly conflicted Bob Mueller, who worked for Obama for 8 years. They won't even look at all of the bad acts and crimes on the other side. A TOTAL WITCH HUNT LIKE NO OTHER IN AMERICAN HISTORY!*

> *Universities will someday study what highly conflicted (and NOT Senate approved) Bob Mueller and his gang of Democratic thugs have done to destroy people. Why is he protecting Crooked Hillary, Comey, McCabe, Lisa Page & her lover, Peter S, and all of his friends on the other side?*

The only "Collusion" is that of the Democrats with Russia and many others. Why didn't the FBI take the Server from the DNC? They still don't have it. Check out how biased Facebook, Google and Twitter are in favor of the Democrats. That's the real Collusion!

I have been told on reliable authority that President Trump had been briefed on my case and that these four tweets were his reaction to what he learned about how the Mueller prosecutors had treated me.

President Trump is right. The FBI never picked up the DNC email server to determine how the DNC emails were stolen. I believe the FBI has refrained from examining this critical evidence because if the FBI and DOJ were honest (and they are not), a legitimate forensic examination of the DNC email server would prove the email theft was an inside job—a leak, not a hack—and that neither Russia nor Guccifer 2.0 had anything to do with the theft.

Seth Rich was killed at 4:30 a.m. EST. The bars in Washington close at 2 a.m. EST. What was Seth Rich doing in the two and a half hours between the bars closing and his heading home that early morning? Reports indicate that Seth Rich was talking on his cellphone when he was assaulted. If this is true, I doubt he was cheating on his girlfriend.

My guess is that Seth Rich was back at the DNC in the hours between 2:00 a.m. and 4:30 a.m. As we have noted, Seth Rich still had his valuables with him when he died, ruling out a typical economically-motivated robbery. But Seth Rich's laptop has never surfaced. If a thumb drive was stolen out of his backpack, who would have known? I'm willing to bet Seth Rich was killed to prevent him from getting to Assange the new cache of DNC emails that he was stealing when he was killed.

But I know from first-hand experience, that Rhee, Zelinsky, and Goldstein—in their determination to grill me for hours on a non-existent source they believe connected me to Assange—these politically motivated prosecutors had zero interest in hearing me explain how the Democrats worked their computers in 2016, or why I believe Seth Rich, not the Russians or Guccifer 2.0—stole both the DNC emails released by Assange on July 22, 2016, as well as the Podesta emails that Assange began releasing on October 7, 2016.

CHAPTER 10

Round Two: More Fear and Loathing

MY HEART FELL when David Gray called me to explain Mueller's Special Counsel had scheduled me to appear a second time before the grand jury on Friday, November 3, 2018. David informed me we would have to leave for Washington on Tuesday, October 30, because Rhee, Zelinsky, and Goldstein wanted to meet with us on Wednesday and Thursday to prepare for the grand jury testimony.

My immediate reaction was that this was now headed to disaster. I was truly exhausted after the first round. Why couldn't Zelinsky and company please be satisfied with the first grand jury appearance? They had testimony from me that they wanted, that's what all the hand-shaking was about in that small conference room at the D.C. federal courthouse. That testimony was "locked in," on the record, such that if I deviated at a trial from what I told the grand jury, that was another way to commit a felony. I had a lot of ways to lose in this increasingly punitive inquisition and almost no ways to win if I couldn't tell Zelinsky what he wanted to hear.

That he wanted a second grand jury appearance meant to me that Zelinsky was determined to get me on the record disclosing who my source to Assange was. Since I knew I did not have a source, I was sure the nightmare would continue. This round, I expected Zelinsky would get even more granular, demanding that I remember more and more details about 2016. The more I thought about 2016, the murkier my memory became. I could no longer distinguish between what I actually remembered from what I remembered today as the way I wanted it to be, or the way I have reconstructed 2016 in my memory given all else that has happened in the two years since then.

I began to feel like I was caught as a character not taking drugs lost in a Hunter S. Thompson "fear and loathing" novel. Only this time, I had the fear and Mueller's henchmen had the loathing. I was becoming increasingly convinced that I was being punished for writing books like "The Obama Nation" and "Where's the Birth Certificate?"—two devastating exposés on Obama that have set the narrative that Obama is a closed communist (partially raised by his mentor Frank Marshall Davis) with cultural sympathy for Islam—a president who was forced to produce a computer printout from 2011 as "proof" Hawaii had authentic 1961 birth records that nobody in the public has ever seen.

Behind Rhee, Zelinsky, and Goldstein, I began to see the Clinton crime syndicate, the Obama mob, and the Soros-funded hard left agenda. Where were we going with this, I asked myself over and over again? If Mueller was trying to break me, I feared he was dangerously close to accomplishing that goal.

I got together with David to plan for the next expensive trip to Washington. Typically, the only reimbursement I got from Mueller's Special Counsel Office for these repeat trips to Washington was one-night's accommodations for me (not for David Gray) at government rates, plus the cost of a round-trip Amtrak ticket.

I was determined to work with David to see if there was a way to avoid having to go back under the third degree with Mueller and company.

"Can we please tell the prosecutors that I have had enough?" I asked David. "I don't think I can go through any more of this."

"If we do that, Mueller will just throw you in front of the grand jury anyway," David explained. "You are still under subpoena and Mueller can force you to take the stand before the grand jury a second time."

"So, what happens then?" I asked.

"You will be forced to answer questions and the grand jury will have an exact transcript of your testimony under oath," David explained. "It will be much more difficult to walk back your grand jury testimony if you make a mistake. At least with the proffer process, you will be in the same type of interviews with Mueller and the FBI as you were before. It will be informal, and we will have a better chance to walk things back."

I went back to asking why I didn't just take the Fifth Amendment. Maybe I should have declined to testify from the beginning.

David reminded me that Mueller could always prosecute me for being a Roger Stone co-conspirator. By cooperating, David felt we had our best chance of remaining a witness.

All that made sense, except I still doubted I could tell Mueller what the prosecutors wanted to hear, and this time I felt Zelinsky would go for broke with the detailed question inquisition about a past I was having an increasingly difficult time remembering.

David and I resolved that our best shot was to ask the prosecutors to give us some of their evidence to review—hopefully the evidence they were planning to quiz me about when they got their hands on me again for what I was beginning to consider round two of a heavy-weight bout between me, three Democratic prosecutors, an army of FBI, and a DOJ/FBI cast of thousands in the unseen background. Yes, I welcomed a chance to "duke it out" with Mueller but not when the deck was stacked against me so that I was sure to lose.

Mueller knew that once Zelinsky could get me to name a source to Assange, my testimony in court would be seen as "ratting" on Stone, "spilling the beans," or some such characterization that would be certain to ruin my future with the conservative movement as an author who could be counted on to conduct exhaustive research and write books that told the truth.

Finally, Zelinsky agreed to send us six pages of my phone records, with three pages from July 26 to August 15, 2016 and three pages from October 3 to October 8, 2016, as a concession to David. The particular selection of these few phone records Mueller chose to share signaled to me that Rhee, Zelinsky, and Goldstein were still looking for someone that I spoke with by telephone to connect me with Assange around my trip to Italy in July and August 2016, and in the second period of October 4 through October 7, 2016, when Assange began dropping the Podesta file.

This was ironic because in one of his outbursts, Zelinsky insisted we would not find my "source" to Assange in my phone records or emails. If this were true, I wondered how Zelinsky imagined I was in touch with this mythical "source"—by smoke signal? So, why now was Zelinsky all of a sudden ready to share phone numbers, unless he planned somehow to trap me? With these phone records, Zelinsky was going more granular, a realization that worried me as I began anticipating hard-driving, detailed questions coming from the prosecutors on every phone call they considered important.

Printing out these pages, I went through the arduous task of identifying each and every phone call, writing in the margins the person I called and my best recollection of the purpose of the phone call. This took most of two days to complete. I realized I was averaging about twenty-five phone calls every day during those time periods, with the records showing a total of approximately three hundred phone calls in total. No wonder I could not remember any given phone call in detail. I was shocked at how busy I had been through the 2016 presidential campaign.

Fortunately, I was successful in identifying all the calls. The next exercise I undertook was to see if there was anyone that I had spoken with by phone in the two time periods now under the microscope.

I noticed that I had talked on the phone with Tom Lipscomb both in July 2016, before I left for Italy, and again in the October 4–7, 2016 period that was the second focus of interest for Zelinsky and the other prosecutors. Lipscomb is a brilliant and well-known investigative reporter and editor in his own right. He is a senior fellow at the Annenberg Center for the Digital Future. He founded "Times Books" for the *New York Times.* I met Tom in 2004 when I was working with John O'Neill and the Swift Boat Veterans for Truth. In 2004, Tom broke several stories on questions about the military records of both John Kerry and George W. Bush. At that time, Tom was publishing in the *Chicago Sun-Times* and the *New York Sun.* While Tom and I have had a cordial professional relationship since 2004, we had an unfortunate falling-out in July 2018.

Tom had a habit of feeding me leads that he had developed from intelligence and other sources that he rarely disclosed to me. At various times, I would take Tom's leads to follow them up myself. From time to time, I was able to publish articles based on research I conducted after Tom fed me the lead. A good example was an email Tom sent me on June 7, 2018. Tom had read my book *Killing the Deep State,* and he knew I was continuing to research the Deep State for a book I was contemplating to write on what was being called "SpyGate"—an apparent coup d'état plan hatched in 2015 by U.S. intelligence officials in conjunction with corrupt Deep State operatives in the DOJ and FBI. I believed the effort had been directed out of the White House by Barack Obama and Valerie Jarrett.

Tom, in his letter of June 7, 2018, was correcting me by directing my attention to British Intelligence.

Tom wrote the following two paragraphs to start his lengthy and detailed memo to me:

> *It was a GCHQ [Government Communications Headquarters, a division of British intelligence] operation designed to suck in the Obama Administration with a shiny toy irresistible to nitwits like Brennan [former head of the CIA under Obama] and Clapper [former Director of National Intelligence under Obama] and get them to drop it at Obama's feet, and it worked like a charm. Comey [former head of the FBI] did just what he was told. And none of it had anything to do with the Hillary Clinton investigation.*

Ever since BREXIT the British Establishment has been trying to undo it, with increasing success locally. Having Trump as POTUS could wreck the whole plan. GCHQ hoped to help defeat him or at least weaken his new regime with a manufactured scandal to keep him busy.

Tom was hinting that SpyGate originated with British Intelligence. His point was as early as 2015, British intelligence concocted the Fusion GPS infamous "Trump Dossier" to create dirt on Trump that could be leaked to the press. Also, under international intelligence agency agreements with the CIA, British intelligence could spy on U.S. citizens, while the CIA and NSA were restricted from doing so. British intelligence then fed their surveillance results and the early drafts of the Fusion GPS dossier with Brennan at CIA and Clapper at DNI.

When the information derived from British intelligence was shared with Obama, the cabal had the ammunition they needed to feed Comey at the FBI. Their goal was to create enough smoke for the DOJ to get FISA electronic surveillance over the Trump campaign. The FISA electronic surveillance was designed to provide corroborating evidence of the "Russia collusion" theory that Hillary and Podesta had created to divert attention from the sloppy cybersecurity maintained by Podesta, Hillary's campaign, and the DNC—as well as to divert attention from the damaging content of the DNC emails being published by WikiLeaks.

Tom's lead was consistent with the information I was developing for my new planned book on SpyGate. The point here is that I realized Tom Lipscomb might have been someone who could have shared with me information he was getting from Assange, or from a source close to Assange. Truthfully, I had no reason to suspect Tom was in contact with Assange, either directly or indirectly, but seeing Tom's phone calls in July when I was preparing to leave for Italy and again in the key period when Assange began dropping the Podesta file in

October 2016, I began to speculate that Tom may have gotten information about WikiLeaks from Peter Smith.

In 2012, Lipscomb introduced me to Peter Smith for the first time. Lipscomb explained that Smith was a multi-millionaire investor in Chicago who lived a double life as a secretive GOP operative. In 2012, Smith called me regularly as I flew as traveling press on Romney's campaign airplane for the last three weeks of the presidential campaign. I remember telling Smith that Romney's crowds were large and enthusiastic. The Romney campaign was working hard to beat Obama in his reelection effort, crisscrossing the country to make three or four different speeches at campaign stops in the battleground states.

I told Smith that I felt Hurricane Sandy may well have cost Romney the election. During the hurricane and the immediate aftermath, Romney took his campaign to Florida, where we rested until the hurricane news subsided. Obama, as president, traveled to New Jersey, one of the states hardest hit by the hurricane, and was photographed embracing Republican Governor Christie while touring the beaches in Atlantic City and promising massive federal aid. That photo opportunity, I believe, cost Governor Christie any chance he may have had of becoming president.

In the 2016 election cycle, Peter Smith came back into my life. My main contact with Smith came in September and October 2016, after I broke the news that Huma Abedin had been sending Hillary's State Department emails to her personal Yahoo email account. This was another case when I connected the dots to figure out a key fact that impacted the 2016 election. How I figured this out goes back to my intel and detective skills. Judicial Watch had released a cache of Huma Abedin emails obtained from a FOIA request. I went through the rather boring exercise of examining each email to make a list of the email addresses involved. I was particularly interested in emails Huma sent using an address *humamabedin@REDACTED.com*. This email address used Huma's middle initial to create a "ama" grouping of letters that had caught my attention. Among the hundreds of email addresses, I found one instance that the government censors had not redacted. That email read: *humamabedin@yahoo.com.* The "yahoo" fill-in met exactly the spaces in the many redacted instances of that email address that I found.

Peter Smith seized on this. He tried to find a legal basis to get Yahoo to release to him the IP addresses of anyone who had accessed Huma's private email account. We realized that Huma was clearly violating national security laws by sending to her private email account Hillary's State Department emails, several of which I identified as containing classified information. We suspected Huma may have shared her username and password with her Muslim Brotherhood friends in the Middle East. When Yahoo refused to give the information to Peter Smith, he and I speculated that if Huma was off-loading Hillary's State Department to her Yahoo account, it was likely she was using a personal computer, not a State Department computer, to archive the emails. This led Peter and me to speculate that Huma used a laptop belonging to her husband, the notorious sexting criminal, the former Democratic congressman Anthony Weiner. Peter convinced his contacts at the New York Police Department to investigate. While we did not know for sure that Weiner was still sexting criminally, we figured sex perverts rarely quit. While FBI Director Comey had already closed down the federal criminal investigation of Hillary's private email server, the NYPD convinced the FBI in New York to join the raid, given the investigation was to catch a sex criminal, not to target Hillary Clinton or Huma Abedin. The rest is history.

I recalled Peter Smith bragging that he was in touch with Assange. While I don't recall ever talking with Peter Smith about what additional DNC material Assange planned to drop after July 22, 2016, I thought it was possible Peter and Lipscomb may have discussed this. Possibly, Lipscomb planted in my brain tips regarding Assange that Lipscomb got from Peter Smith. As I illustrated above, Lipscomb had a habit of planting information and investigate leads with me without disclosing his sources.

When David Gray let Zelinsky know I was examining this line of inquiry, Zelinsky was dismissive. "I don't want to waste time with Corsi sending up trial balloons," Zelinsky insisted. This was a constant Zelinsky refrain. Mueller's prosecutors wanted me to remember what I could not remember. Zelinsky blew up when I tried to refresh my memory by reconstructing 2016 from the minimal information I had. Peter Smith died on May 14, 2017, in a suspicious suicide in a hotel room in Rochester, Minnesota. Zelinsky also objected to David Gray that he did not want me "trying to pin this on some dead guy."

Reviewing these phone records, I also realize that Tom Lipscomb was connected to Total Banking Solutions, a New Jersey company that worked with banks nationwide. Given my extensive former career in financial services, Tom introduced me to the TBS principals and I agreed to accept a consulting contract with the company. TBS was in the business of brokering deposit accounts. Given the FDIC insurance limit of $250,000 per depositor, TBS had developed a multi-million-dollar business taking large deposits, typically in the hundreds of thousands or millions of dollars and breaking them up into $250,000 pieces. The various pieces were then distributed among as many banks as it took. I considered this a circumvention of the spirit of the FDIC laws and I suggested to the TBS principals that we might go to London to see if we could get private insurance to cover larger deposits—a strategy that would obviate the need to break jumbo deposits into these 250-thousand-dollar chunks.

I involved Ted Malloch in the project. Ted had top connections with international insurance broker Willis Towers Watson, just as Ted had top level connections with PricewaterhouseCoopers. We planned a trip to London with TBS that was scheduled to take place immediately after Election Day in the United States, November 8, 2016. Ultimately, the project failed because TBS could get FDIC insurance over their thousands of 250,000 deposits at cut-rate government rates, compared to the private insurance that turned out to be costlier. I still consider my solution will be necessary should the public become aware of the billions of dollars in $250,000 size deposits that are brokered by TBS and its competitor companies among commercial banks in the United States. I doubt Congress is aware of the burdens this tactic places on FDIC, given that the TBS system by-passes the deposit limits Congress has put in place.

The genius behind the Total Banking Solutions is Dennis Santiago, the company's Senior Managing Director for Compliance and Analytics. During the Reagan administration, Dennis worked as a strategic warfare systems designer, missile defense architect, and arms control analyst. He has twenty-eight years of experience in the finance industry plus ten years in the aerospace-defense industry. For TBS, Dennis invented the company's Bank Monitor, a system that tests the safety and soundness of 100 percent of all depository institutions in the United States. Dennis' model allows TBS to rate the safety of financial institutions into which the downsized $250,000 packages of deposits are to be placed. The TBS Bank Monitor is used by the financial industry, as well as federal and state agencies to assist in monitoring the systemic health of the U.S. banking system. In meetings with Lipscomb and me, Dennis showed a keen interest in Assange and I recall speculating with him what Assange's next steps might be in the period after July 22, 2016.

I mention TBS because my phone records reflected a forty-seven minute phone call with Lipscomb on October 5, 2016. I figured the prosecutors might have suspected Lipscomb and I were discussing Assange. But then, I realized that later that day, I had scheduled a conference call with Total Banking Solutions to discuss the trip to London to meet with insurance agency Willis and Lloyds of London. Tom Lipscomb had an agreement with me and TBS to share in the revenue should we be able to get a deal together with TBS, and Willis and Lloyds. Ted Malloch also had an agreement to share in the revenue for arranging the Willis and Lloyds meetings in London. My notes reflected that Ted Malloch attended this conference call, but Tom Lipscomb and Dennis Santiago did not.

In truth, I do not believe Tom Lipscomb, Peter Smith, or Dennis Santiago had a direct link with Assange and I see no reason to think Lipscomb or Santiago were feeding me with information they derived from Assange. In September and October 2016, everyone concerned about presidential politics was talking about Assange and whether or not Assange would provide the "October Surprise" against Hillary. Assange had telegraphed to the world after July 22, 2016, that he had more DNC emails and that the emails, when made public, would be devastating to Hillary Clinton's presidential campaign. It was inevitable that Lipscomb, Santiago, and I would be speculating about Assange, given our mutual interest in seeing Donald Trump win the presidency. Even if one or more of us did have a link to Assange—which I do not believe was the case—I could see no crime even if we had shared information Assange had given us.

In analyzing the phone records, I also saw a series of calls that involved an article I was writing for WND.com on Libya. Here is the sequence of the calls and the explanation of the calls that I wrote up for David Gray to send to the Special Counsel:

- On October 4, 2016, at 10:08 a.m. EST, I phoned Art Moore (the WND editor who generally edited stories I submitted to publication for WND).

- At that time, I was working on a story about Hillary Clinton's involvement in covert arms sales to Libya, specifically regarding Marc Turi—an arms dealer who was under criminal investigation at that time for arranging arms sales involving Libya and Turkey.

- As I recall I had been provided videos to support the story by JoAnne Holzgang Moriarty—JoAnne and her husband James were frequent sources for me on stories about Libya. JoAnne and her husband had been involved in Libya in the oil business, prior to the fall of Qaddafi. The videos were rough originals provided JoAnne by her Libyan sources.

- On October 4, 2016, at 10:27 a.m., I phoned Art Moore a second time and we had a five-minute conversation.

- On October 4, 2016, at 10:32 a.m., I phoned Robert Unruh, the WND assignments editor, for a two-minute conversation.

- On October 4, 2016, at 12:12 p.m., JoAnne Holzgang Moriarty phoned me for a four-minute conversation—I believe this had to be about the Libya article.

- On October 4, 2016, at 12:57 p.m., I participated for eighteen minutes in the WND daily editorial.

- On October 4, 2016, at 1:33 p.m., I called Conrad Tice, a WND Assistant Producer who worked from Johnstown, Pennsylvania. Conrad Tice was a WND editor who worked on editing videos. I'm fairly certain this involved editing the Libyan videos I had received from JoAnne to include in the Marc Turi article.

On October 4, 2016, at 3:04 p.m., Art Moore sent me an email (he copied *stories@worldnetdaily.com*—the email address to which stories were submitted for editing). Art Moore's email read: "Jerry, I'll insert this story about Marc Turi in the three-video story for tonight. But it obviously deserves further reporting, i.e., what Turi knows about Clinton's effort to arm the anti-Qaddafi rebels."

On October 4, 2016, at 6:09 p.m., Art Moore sent me a second email that read: "The angle would be that Obama's DOJ apparently dropped the charges (against Marc Turi) to protect Hillary one month before the election. So, what were they afraid Turi would reveal if they went to discovery and trial?"

On October 5, 2016, at 10:31 a.m., I received a phone call from JoAnne Holzgang Moriarty that I recall inquiring about the status of the Libya article.

On October 5, at 12:30 p.m., I phoned Perkins Coie in Phoenix, Arizona, to contact Marc Turi's lawyer. The call lasted two minutes and I left a message.

On October 5, 2016, at 12:32 p.m., I phoned Judge Napolitano at Fox News. Judge Napolitano was a source I was planning to quote in the Libya story. The call lasted two minutes and I left a message.

On October 5, 2016, at 12:46 p.m., I phoned Robert Unruh to brief him on my phone calls to Perkins Coie and to Judge Napolitano.

On October 5, 2016, at 12:52 p.m., I emailed Art Moore, saying: "I have calls in to Turi's lawyer and to Judge Napolitano at Fox. No response yet."

On October 5, 2016, at 3:11 p.m., I emailed Art Moore saying, "I just interviewed Judge Napolitano and will have the story done by 6:00 p.m. today on Marc Turi."

On October 5, 2016, at 4:31 p.m., I emailed Judge Napolitano, sending him a draft of my Marc Turi story for corrections. The email read: "JUDGE: Please make any changes you want. If you could, please make the changes in RED so I can see them easily. Also, please note that I do not write headlines. WND has a headlines editor—my headlines as submitted are merely suggestions."

On October 5, 2016, at 4:39 p.m., Judge Napolitano emailed me saying, "All good. See my proper Fox title below. I am also Distinguished Visiting Professor of Law at Brooklyn Law School. Judge Napolitano, not Justice Napolitano. I don't know if the Rogers made a fortune, but they certainly earned money from all this."

On October 5, 2016, at 5:12 p.m., I emailed Judge Napolitano, saying: "Thanks I will make these changes."

On October 6, 2016, at 9:18 a.m., I emailed Judge Napolitano a copy of the article, thanking him. The article had been published by WND under my by-line with the title: "Judge Napolitano: Case exposes Hillary's 'secret war.'" The subtitle as published by WND read, "DOJ dropped charges against Libyan arms dealer to protect Clinton."

JoAnne and James Moriarty phoned me just after I prepared this phone call analysis for Mueller. JoAnne and James explained to me that two FBI agents from the Special Prosecutor showed up at their doorstep, accompanied by the local sheriff. The FBI grilled JoAnne and James for three hours, they reported to me—interviewing them separately, not together. JoAnne and James explained to me that the main interest for the FBI was to determine if I had been a source for Julian Assange or if I had any connection with WikiLeaks.

JoAnne and James explained that the source of my many articles on Libya were Libyan tribesmen who were in exile in Egypt and that I had become a hero with the people of Libya for explaining how much the Libyan tribes have suffered at the hands of Secretary of State Clinton. JoAnne and James made it clear that I was not a source for Julian Assange and that we had never discussed WikiLeaks in our work on Libya.

I subsequently learned that the FBI also visited Tom Lipscomb. Given our estrangement that dated to July 2018, Lipscomb did not call me to let him know the FBI had visited with him in October. Knowing Tom, my guess is that Tom told the FBI that he had no ties to Assange or to WikiLeaks, and that he had no reason to believe I had ties either.

What surprised me was the realization that I was still under investigation by the FBI. These visits confirmed to me that Rhee, Zelinsky, and Goldstein still refused to accept that I figured out accurately in August 2016 that Assange had Podesta's emails and that he would release them in serial fashion starting in October that year. Clearly, the FBI had found this sequence of calls suspicious, especially with me placing a call to Perkins Coie, the law firm that represented both Hillary Clinton's campaign and the DNC during the 2016 presidential campaign.

I also saw that on October 7, 2016, I had three phone calls with Roger Stone. As I recall, Roger was concerned that Assange should be alerted to the fact the Billy Bush story was about to break. I told the FBI that my best recollection was that I told Roger that I would make an effort to get this word out to Assange, though I knew I had no direct or indirect link that could communicate this word to Assange.

David Gray put me on notice that a press release during the morning of October 7, 2016 had announced to the world in advance that the Billy Bush tape would be dropped that day. I recall that Roger had made it clear to me the Billy Bush tape would have recorded Trump bragging about grabbing women by their genitals.

In the notes I sent to David for Mueller detailing my recollection of the phone calls, I noted the following:

- On October 7, 2016, at 11:27 p.m., I phoned Roger Stone in Washington, D.C., for one minute. While I have no specific recollection of the call, I believe the discussion was about the status of the Wikileaks publication of the Podesta emails and Roger's concern that Assange should start publishing immediately the Podesta emails.

- My next call on October 7, 2016, was at 1:08 p.m. to participate in the daily WND conference call. The call lasted eighteen minutes and according to my best recollection, I briefed the WND staff on Roger Stone's urgency to get Assange to start publishing the Podesta emails. I believe this was the WND editorial meeting when I asked WND staff attending the editorial meeting if anyone had a contact where they could reach Assange to urge him to start publishing the Podesta emails.

- On October 7, 2016, Roger Stone phoned me at 1:42 p.m. for eighteen minutes. While I have no specific recall of the details of the conversation, I'm sure Roger was anxious to know if I had reached Assange. I believe told Roger I asked the WND staff for assistance. I recall also telling Roger that I had posted tweets with #Assange and @Assange to urge Assange to publish. FBI Agent Myers in Quantico should have my tweets—I have been unable to recover my tweets from that period.

- My next call was at 2:00 p.m. with TBS to discuss Lloyds and our planned trip to London after the election. As I recall,

ABC, XYZ, and Dennis Santiago participated in the conference call for TBS. I do not recall if Malloch attended the
conference call.

- On October 7, 2016, at 2:18 p.m., I called Roger Stone for a
  twenty-one minute call. Again, I don't have a specific recollection of the discussion, but I feel sure it involved Assange and
  Billy Bush. In the course of these three calls, I believe I made
  clear to Roger Stone that I had no way to contact Assange
  directly and I do not recall having any source who I knew to
  be in contact with Assange.

In our subsequent discussions with Mueller's prosecutors in Washington, this sequence turned out to be problematic because I could
not remember if I had told both the WND and the TBS conference
calls that day about the Billy Bush tape. Mueller's henchmen again
accused me of lying when they informed my memory that Malloch
could have attended the TBS conference call was incorrect because
Malloch was on a trans-Atlantic intercontinental flight at that time.

The FBI had the resources to research details like this in advance
and, despite my repeated pleas that my memory was vague at best
on these events, the FBI held me to a standard that every one of my
answers had to be precisely correct, or I would be accused of lying.
Truthfully, seeing my phone records in 2018 was the first time I
recalled anything about these phone calls from 2016, and even then,
I was doing what Zelinsky called "reconstruction."

Before we headed back to Washington for the second grand jury
appearance, David Gray had a phone conference with Rhee, Zelinsky,
and Goldstein. David reported to me that in this conference call,
Zelinsky had come across very aggressively.

"Tell Doctor Corsi that we are giving him one final chance to
come back here to this time stop lying to us," Zelinsky said. "Our
patience with him is getting razor thin."

This alarmed me. What about all those congratulatory hand-shakes with the prosecutors and the FBI following my first grand jury appearance? If I was lying then, it was hard to understand why Zelinsky shook my hand and say, "Not bad for an Ignatius man."

Rhee tried to moderate Zelinsky's aggressiveness by telling David that I had given them the impression that I was often "confused." That was accurate, but more precisely, I was scared to death Zelinsky would press me on something out of the blue—something Zelinsky would spring on me to throw me off balance so he could see how I would respond.

"Doctor Corsi's testimony before the grand jury was pivotal to us from any number of perspectives," Rhee said, again moderating Zelinsky's anger. "But we are having difficulty with the conflicting stories he keeps remembering."

I repeatedly told Rhee, Zelinsky, and Goldstein that 2016 was two years ago and I did not remember it in detail. I found I could recall almost nothing from any particular email or phone call. When I finally opened my 2016 emails, I was startled by how much I had forgotten. The exercise with the eight pages of phone records was the same.

My conclusion was that Rhee, Zelinsky, and Goldstein felt like they had the cat in the bag in the moments after I finished testifying to the grand jury. They acted like they were ready to pop champagne. But when they took that testimony upstairs to Mueller, they were rebuked.

In round one, Rhee, Zelinsky, and Goldstein had failed to establish that I had a source to Assange. Lacking this, the evidence I provided against Stone was very weak. So, what if we had concocted a cover story to explain away Stone's "Podesta's time in the barrel" email. How many lies had Hillary Clinton told in her two attempts to run for the president? So, what if Roger Stone used my cover story to testify before the House Intelligence Committee. Roger could amend that testimony and Congress rarely pursues anyone for criminal charges of perjury.

Without the link to Assange, there was no "Russian Collusion" that could be pinned on Roger Stone. That's why I was headed back to the grand jury. I expected the next round would press my memory to the breaking point.

I felt this was rapidly becoming an adversarial process, not the type of cooperation I expected to give Mueller's Special Counsel office.

Rather than looking at documents to try to figure them out, I felt the process was rapidly becoming confrontational. What put me further on edge was Zelinsky's perception that I was "lying."

My intent from the beginning had been to tell the truth. Why otherwise would I have handed over my computers, my cellphone, my emails and everything else?

What was clear to me now was that the Special Prosecutor ability to examine every detail of my reporting, my business dealings, my communications with my wife—certainly more detail than I myself remembered.

Even when my memories were vague, Rhee, Zelinsky, and Goldstein could bore down for specific responses, in minute detail, aided by an endless budget and an army of FBI investigators ready to be sent into the field on a moment's notice.

We need to cover one final point. The prosecutors also told David Gray that I had deleted emails on or around October 11, 2018. Their suspicion appeared to be that at Roger Stone's instruction, I had deleted emails that would have shown I contacted Assange, either directly or indirectly, regarding the Billy Bush video.

I could not remember having done this and I'm sure I had no way to contact Assange in October 2016, or at any other time. But I decided to reload my laptop from the Time Machine for October 1, 2016, the only date saved by the Time Machine prior to October 11, 2016. Following that, I planned to reload October 18, 2016, from the Time Machine, the first date saved after October 11, 2016.

I struggled for hours and finally managed on October 28, 2016, to reload the laptop from October 1, 2016. But then, when I tried to reload October 18, 2016, the laptop finally died. I could not get the laptop to reboot successfully.

The result was that once again I would have to return to the Special Counsel without having the opportunity to see the data that I was certain to be grilled about. Even worse, the prosecutors told David that Quantico had been able to restore the deleted emails. So, the prosecutors and the FBI would again know what they were looking for and I would be in the dark when questioned.

CHAPTER 11

The Mueller Inquisition Blows Up

November 22, 2018

On Wednesday, October 31, 2018, David Gray and I met again with Rhee, Zelinsky, and Goldstein, along with their army of FBI agents in the windowless conference within the unmarked FBI building in southeast Washington. This routine was definitely getting old.

Rhee and Goldstein led off, evidently implementing a good-cop/bad-cop strategy the prosecutors evidently had decided to use.

"We appreciate your cooperation," Goldstein began.

"We are only interested in the truth," Rhee continued, repeating her constant refrain. "We appreciate you are better at reconstructing than remembering. But since we are only after the truth, just tell us when you can't remember."

Here we go again, I thought to myself. If only it were that simple. When I cannot remember something, the prosecutors' rejoinder that they do not understand how I could not remember that. When I struggle to remember, I risk reconstructing incorrectly. Then I'm accused of lying.

"It frustrates me that I can't remember," I responded. "And then, sometimes I wonder whether I am reconstructing or inventing. Sometimes I can't tell if I remembered or invented."

"We are not trying to plant suggestions," Goldstein insisted.

"We need to know when you are reconstructing and when we have jogged your memory such that you are remembering," Rhee added.

By now, I was totally confused. "My mind is becoming a mental mish-mash," I explained. "I don't have all my emails, or my phone records. You don't show me the evidence you have. When I give you my current memory and it differs from some piece of evidence you have, you say I am lying. You want me to remember accurately what happened two years ago, and I have told you repeatedly that I am not capable of doing that."

I felt this discussion was only getting me more confused. What I imagined my cooperation would be was very different from this. In the type of investigative reporting I have done for years, we are always digging for facts. There is always discussion about how to interpret events and what we dig up. There is no penalty for misinterpreting the facts or for getting the facts wrong in this often robust and contentious editorial discussion. It always takes a give-and-take between authors such as me and editors. But my goal and the goal of my editors at WND.com was always to get to the bottom of it, to discover the truth.

These people wanted precise answers to events from two years ago which I am unable to remember with precision regarding any particular email or phone call in 2016. The way Mueller had set up this inquisition was bound to fail with me. I was rapidly losing the ability to distinguish between remembering, reconstructing, and inventing. The more detailed their questions were, the more pressure I felt under.

When Rhee and Goldstein were finished, Zelinsky jumped in. That morning, Zelinsky looked angry, completely pissed off. He had a frown that would not quit, and his tone of voice was sharp.

David Gray's notes taken during the interview show Zelinsky was prepared to fire off a series of questions, all aimed at digging deeper into my supposed relationship with Assange. This was rapidly becoming a nightmare.

Here are just a sample of the seemingly hundreds of questions Zelinsky shot at me, which I had to recall to the best of my ability because I had no notes or documents in front of me and Zelinsky provided me none of the copious documents the Special Prosecutor possessed to refresh my memory:

- "What did Roger Stone understand about your relationship with Julian Assange?"

- "What conversations were you having with Roger Stone after July 22, 2016?"

- "Let's go back to Stone's email of July 25, 2016—the 'Get to Assange' email you passed on to Malloch. Prior to this email, what reason had you given to Stone that he would think you could get to Assange?"

- "Did you and Malloch discuss Nigel Farage or any of the others in the United Kingdom involved with Brexit? Were these people a channel to Assange?"

- "As far as Roger Stone was concerned, did he think Malloch would produce? Did he think Malloch would go see Assange?"

- "Had you told Roger Stone your assessment that Malloch had one of the best Rolodex contact lists of influential people worldwide? Did you tell Stone that Malloch was politically connected in the United Kingdom?"

We went on like that for more than an hour, with Rhee jumping in from time to time to tag-team the aggressive line of detailed questioning Zelinsky was pursuing. Many of the questions Zelinsky and Rhee were shooting at me involved me knowing what Roger Stone or Malloch thought.

In a courtroom, these questions would have been ruled out-of-bounds over a "state-of-mind" objection. I cannot be asked to answer what someone else was thinking. I wanted to explain to Zelinsky and

Rhee that if they wanted to know what Roger Stone, Ted Malloch, Nigel Farage, or anybody else was thinking, they should ask them.

I now had no doubt that I was being called back because Mueller had yelled at Rhee, Zelinsky, and Goldstein for letting me off the hook at my first grand jury appearance by not asking me under oath to identify my "source" with Assange.

My attempts to explain how the Democrats' computer system was set up, or why I was convinced Seth Rich, not the Russians, had stolen the DNC emails fell on deaf ears. Mueller's henchmen were locked into their conclusions that the Russians stole the DNC emails and that Stone coordinated with Assange in a Putin-Trump plot to drop the emails so as to destroy Hillary's 2016 campaign. The prosecutors were closed-minded on this and the problem was that I refused to fit into their Procrustean bed.

Late in the afternoon, Goldstein showed me a key document. It was an email I had written from Italy to Roger Stone in August 2016. Goldstein would not permit us to make a copy, but from memory, what I remember the email as saying was, "Word is…Assange will make two drops, one soon on Clinton Foundation, second one in October on Podesta." The email was not that clear, but that was the gist of what it said.

I had no recollection whatsoever of writing that email, but if the prosecutors had it, I assumed it had to be authentic. Reading it that day in the windowless conference room, it occurred to me that I was placating Roger Stone. As you will recall, I believed Roger Stone had to have a source to Assange other than me simply because during August 2016, Roger was always insistent that Assange would drop material on the Clinton Foundation. I always doubted this. Assange had made clear in numerous interviews that the DNC emails he had ready to go public after July 22, 2016, would have a devastating effect on Hillary.

Charles Ortel and I had published extensively about the Clinton Foundation crimes. I even wrote a book in 2016, titled: "Partners in Crime: The Clintons' Scheme to Monetize the White House for Personal Gain." The Clinton Foundation involved a massive, global financial scam in which the Clintons had scammed a charity, raising money on earthquakes and other disasters, in order to enrich themselves.

But the problem was that detecting the fraud required an expert ability to read audited financial reports and that skill required the expertise of someone like Charles Ortel—a well-respected Wall Street financial analyst. For the average person, understanding the full magnitude of the Clintons' crimes perpetrated through the shell-game of the Clinton Foundation was difficult, if not impossible.

While I doubted Assange would think new Clinton Foundation material would derail Hillary's campaign, I decided to placate Roger. So, I invented that Assange would drop Clinton Foundation material in order that Roger would listen to me that Assange really had Podesta emails that Assange planned to start making public in October.

I knew there was no way Rhee, Zelinsky, or Goldstein would buy that explanation, despite the fact I believed it to be true. That was my best reconstruction on seeing yet another email that I did not recall writing.

On August 15, 2016, I wrote an article in WND.com for Roger Stone, titled "Trump Adviser: WikiLeaks Plotting Email Dump to Derail Hillary." In the first paragraph of that article, I explained that Stone was claiming his computer and personal bank accounts were hacked in retaliation for declaring publicly he believes Julian Assange has a complete set of Hillary Clinton's thirty-thousand scrubbed "private emails" and was preparing to release them to derail Hillary's campaign. In the second paragraph, I reported that in an interview I conducted with Stone, he claimed he had communicated directly with Assange.

On August 8, 2016, Stone gave a speech to the Southwest Broward Republican Organization in which he claimed, "I actually have communicated with Assange. I believe the next tranche of his documents pertain to the Clinton Foundation but there's no telling what the October surprise may be."

In August 2016, based on my interview with Stone and on this speech, I believed Stone had been in touch with Assange through someone other than me. As I pointed out earlier, I always wondered how accurate Stone's contact with Assange was, since Stone was claiming Assange had either emails from Hillary Clinton's thirty-thousand scrubbed emails or documents regarding the Clinton Foundation. My recollection is that by the time I returned to the United States from Italy, on August 12, 2016, I had figured out that the DNC emails Assange had yet to drop belonged to Podesta.

Mueller's henchmen grew irritated every time I tried to explain to them that I never thought Stone believed I had a direct contact to Assange, and I'm not sure Stone believed my claim in this new "word is…" email that I wrote to him from Italy. But, at the same time, I thought Stone had someone other than me who connected him to Assange. It was not until his famous tweet of August 21, 2016, that I thought Stone had come around to understand I was right.

This was confirmed when Stone final produced text messages to support Stone's claim that New York radio show host Randy Credico was the source connecting him to Assange. On August 27, 2016, Credico wrote to Stone, "Julian Assange has kryptonite on Hillary." Then on September 29, 2016, Credico wrote, "You are not going to drag my name into this are you?" Finally, on October 1, 2016, Credico wrote to Stone, "Big News Wednesday." To this, Credico added, "Now pretend u don't know me."[46]

Clearly, Credico wanted to keep his name out of the controversy. But the discovery of these emails November 2018 confirmed what

---

46   Ross, Chuck. "Bombshell Text Messages Support Roger Stone's Claims About WikiLeaks Backchannel," Daily Caller, November 14, 2018. *https://dailycaller.com/2018/11/14/roger-stone-wikileaks-randy-credico-mueller/.*

Stone told the House Intelligence Committee in October 2017—namely that Credico was his back-channel to Assange. Never once has Stone claimed that I was the source connecting him to Assange. While I believe Stone took my intuitive deductions as interesting, including my conclusions stated in the "word is…" email from Italy in August 2016, I doubt Stone ever felt I had a connection to Assange.

But for Rhee, Zelinsky, and Goldstein, the "word is…" email was a big deal, triggering another barrage of questions.

- "Why did you say "word is…" to Stone? Were you trying to imply you had a source to Assange?"

- "Were you just promoting your importance to Stone by bragging that you knew what Assange was going to do? Did you write the email to make it look like you were somehow on the inside of Assange's circle, or had been tipped off about what Assange was going to do?"

- "Were you trying to promote yourself to Trump through Stone. Were you puffing or embellishing?"

- "Do you remember ever confessing to Stone that you had no contact with Assange?"

- "Were you trying with this memo to represent to Stone that you had a source connected with Assange?"

- "Did you want Stone to believe you had inside information?"

- "Did you ever say to Stone that you did not have a connection to Assange?"

- "Why did you have the impression Stone had a different source than you? Why won't you admit you were the source for Stone?"

- "What was the purpose of the cover-up? What did Stone think was the purpose of the cover-up? Did he ever tell you why he wanted you to write about Podesta? What did you think was the purpose of the cover-up?"

- "Why did you want to talk to Roger Stone when you returned from Italy? Do you have any actual recollection of the conversation you had with Stone on August 15, 2016?"

- "When Roger asks you on August 30, 2016, to write the Podesta memo, what did he tell you?"

- "Did Stone tell you he was going to attach your Podesta memo to his prepared testimony before the House Intelligence Committee?"

- "Why didn't you object when you found out Stone had used your memo in his House Intelligence Committee testimony?"

- "What did Stone ask you about Malloch after Malloch was detained and questioned at Boston Logan Airport?'

- "Was Stone worried that Malloch might blow the cover story? What do you remember about your conversation with Roger after you spoke with Malloch over Malloch's wife's phone?"

This was all getting extremely tiresome.

I began asking for a break to confer with my attorney after almost every question I was beginning to have a hard time understanding the questions, let alone figuring out the answers.

Every time I asked for a break, the three prosecutors and the FBI army gathered all their materials and marched out of the room. After a while, it began to look to me like a comedy routine."

"I'm sorry to make you do this," I said, watching them. "You guys can stay here, and David and I can go to the conference room next door," I suggested.

"No, Doctor Corsi, we are used to this," Zelinsky explained. "This is our job."

At another point, I complained to Zelinsky that the questioning was getting tedious.

"Much of what I do is tedious, Doctor Corsi," Zelinsky answered in a way that suggested to me he was saying that while his lawyering job was tedious, he was good at it.

I began to feel Zelinsky was beginning to treat me like the cat who had caught the bird and was determined to torment it a while before eating it.

At another point, I asked Zelinsky if the eight-inch binder with my name on it from which he was drawing exhibits to question me was all about me. It frightened me to think just how much evidence on me the Special Prosecutor had accumulated on me. I was beginning to think Zelinsky knew more about me than I did.

"I'm not going to tell you if this binder is about you," Zelinsky answered me with a smirk. "And I'm not going to tell you how many more binders like this that I have."

On and on, Rhee, Zelinsky, and Goldstein went. They became equally granular on the cover-up articles I wrote for Stone, allowing Stone to attribute his "Podesta's time in the barrel" to the payments John and Tony Podesta received from Russia.

- "When first did you discuss with Stone the need for a cover-up?"

- "What was the purpose of the cover-up? Do you have any actual memory of Stone telling you what to write?"

- "When Stone said that tweet was based on information from Corsi, was that true?"

- "Do you have any memory of Stone talking to you about Peter Schweizer's piece on Russia? Do you recall Roger telling you to do research or to get intelligence on Podesta's activities in Russia? What did Roger say? When did he say it? Do you remember, or is that an impression?

- "When Roger asked you on August 30, 2016, to write a background memo on Podesta, what did he tell you? Do you remember after getting the instruction from Roger to write the memo, if you were surprised about the request? What were you thinking at the time?"

- "You told Roger that Assange was going to release Podesta's emails in serial fashion. Did you tell that to Roger on or before August 31, 2016? What exactly did you say to Roger about Podesta releasing the Podesta emails in day-by-day fashion?"

- "On October 12, 2016, Podesta accused Stone of having advance knowledge of Assange and the emails. What research did you do around Podesta's claim that Roger had advance knowledge?"

- "Do you have any memory of Stone actually telling you what to write?"

- "Did you ever tell Roger there was nothing to hide? Did you ever tell Roger what you are telling us?"

Rhee, Zelinsky, and Goldstein spent hours interrogating me over and over on every email and phone call I made in 2016. I thought we would never get through 2016, but I also know the prosecutors were interested in my interaction with Stone in 2017 and in 2018. I thought I was going to have to be taken out of the interrogation room, collapsed, on a stretcher. The sessions were going from 10 a.m. to 6 p.m. or later. The prosecutors took breaks and left the building for lunch. But David and I stayed in the windowless conference room, concerned the photographers outside would turn seeing us into a circus. My stomach was in such knots that I was unable to eat lunch.

David Gray's copious notes taken virtually word-for-word at the time are filled with my protests that I didn't remember, that I had only vague recollections of these events, that I couldn't recall precisely what I was thinking in a given conversation or around a particular press report. "I don't recall that discussion with Roger," I protested. "It was late at night."

But Rhee and especially Zelinsky kept repeating the same questions in slightly different form, wanting to know details of conversations and emails that I couldn't remember.

Here we were in the second round, going over 2016 again and again, with Rhee, Zelinsky, and Goldstein drilling deeper to find out what I was thinking, what Roger was thinking, who said what to whom, what were we planning, etc. Finally, I was reduced to saying things like, "I have a definite impression that happened, but I don't remember." I was starting to make no sense, not even to myself. I became tired and confused under this rapid-fire questioning about events two years ago.

Even more frustrating, Rhee, Zelinsky, and Goldstein, by their tone of voice, the displeasure on their faces, their body language, managed to communicate to me that they refused to accept my recollection that I figured out Assange had Podesta's emails. They refused to accept my impression that Stone did not believe I had been in touch with Assange. They refused to accept to accept my impression that Stone had contacts to Assange other than me. Rhee, Zelinsky, and Goldstein wanted to make me Roger Stone's co-conspirator, his secret link to Assange.

Goldstein burst out, "Our patience with you, Doctor Corsi, is wearing very thin. I'm warning you." Zelinsky alternately looked angry and started hurling at me heated questions in rapid-fire fashion. At other times, he looked bored. Finally, he started yawning. "Am I boring you, Mr. Zelinsky?" I asked. "Maybe you need a break."

The prosecutors wanted to know why I didn't go to London to see Assange, as Joseph Farah wanted me to do. After all, I went to Kenya to search for Obama's birth certificate. It was pointless, but I wanted to explain I went to Kenya in 2008—I was ten years younger then—and I was nearly thrown into a Kenyan prison. I didn't want to be at risk some intelligence agency either in the U.S. or in the U.K. might place me under surveillance the minute I tried to see Assange.

I tried to explain under Supreme Court decisions like the Pentagon Papers case, I was sure that as a journalist, I had a right to see Assange, even if Assange were in possession of stolen emails and even if the stolen emails contained classified information (which they did not).

But when I brought up the Pentagon Papers case, Zelinsky shot back, "We know all about *New York Times v. U.S.*, Doctor Corsi." Right, I should have realized, they were the super lawyers from Yale, while to them, I was just an aging Ph.D. from Harvard who made the mistake of being conservative and was stupid enough to support Donald Trump.

The prosecutors did not want to hear about Seth Rich, about Tom Lipscomb and Peter Smith, or anybody else—just Roger Stone and Assange, Roger Stone and Assange, Roger Stone and Assange.

They wanted me to admit that I was Roger Stone's "source." They pressed me to admit I knew Roger Stone was covering up not only for him, but also for me (because I told him Assange had Podesta's emails). Truthfully, the thought had never occurred to me that Roger would think he had to cover for me because I knew I had no contact with Assange and I believe Roger thought I had no contact with Assange. There was nothing for me to cover up. I was telling the truth, but that didn't help, not in a universe where Rhee, Zelinsky, and Goldstein had pre-determined the answers to every question they asked. My problem was that I was trying to tell the truth and what I felt was the truth was not what they wanted to hear.

If Roger had thought I made contact with Assange, Roger would have wanted me to share the contact. Roger would have been happy to take my contact and use it for himself, with my permission—permission I'm sure I would have given him.

David Gray correctly advised me, "If you don't tell them you were Stone's 'source' for information from Assange, these guys will put you in prison. You can see they don't like you."

I wasn't sure what anybody meant saying I was Stone's "source" for Assange. Chuck Ross of the Daily Caller finally found two tweets I posted around his press conference in London Assange scheduled for October 4, 2016. On October 2, 2016, I tweeted: "If Assange has the goods on Hillary, he ought just to drop the goods. Otherwise, he's going to make a fool of himself." Then on October 4, 2016, after Assange cancelled the press conference, I tweeted, "So Assange made a fool of himself. Had zero, or he would have released it. Will take grassroots on internet to get the truth out to beat Hillary."

Chuck Ross correctly interpreted these two tweets as indicating that I had no knowledge from Assange or from any connected to Assange regarding what emails Assange had and when he was going to make them public. My "figuring it out" connecting the dots could easily have been interpreted as speculating, not knowing.

The next two days with Rhee, Zelinsky, and Goldstein were total hell for me.

The Gestapo, the KGB, the communist Chinese during the Korean War, all used the same questioning techniques as Mueller. The same questions with minor variations are asked over and over. Any minor differences in a response, due to memory lapses, are thrown back at the person under interrogation as examples of "lies." The questioning gets more granular, demanding the person under interrogation must remember what everyone said in conversations, telephone calls, or written communications such as emails. Next, the grand inquisitors demand to know what you were thinking and what others are thinking. Claims you cannot remember are taken as intentional memory lapses designed to protect you or others. You are constantly threatened with being imprisoned for the rest of your life. Eventually, you cannot distinguish reconstructions of the past, from inventing recollections, from actual memories. Finally, you beg just to tell Mueller's henchmen what they want to hear. This they reject because what they wanted was you to confess to them what they wanted to hear.

This is exactly what happened to me.

One of the most memorable moments from the inquisition came when Jeannie Rhee decided to be sympathetic. She put on her kindest face and explained we were going to do an exercise.

"Let's say, Doctor Corsi, that there are three categories," she began. "This first category are things about which you have a distinct memory. This second category are things you can vaguely remember but cannot recall in any detail. The third category are things you cannot remember at all."

I agreed to go along. Pleased that I agreed to go along, Rhee began asking me about specific emails, specific conversations, specific events. Pretty soon, I found I had expanded her three categories into nine categories. There were questions where I had a distinct memory, but then there were times I suspect my distinct memory was a reconstruction, or I suspected the distinct memory was an invention. I had become unable to tell if I remembered anything correctly, or if all my memories were reconstructions, or even made-up inventions. I had the same problem with vague items and items I couldn't remember—maybe I was reconstructing something to be vague or inventing something to be vague.

Finally, Rhee grew exasperated. She showed me two emails about which she had been questioning me. "Doctor Corsi, do you actually remember these emails?" she asked.

"I'm sorry," I answered. "I had forgotten all about them until you showed then to me today."

Rhee gave up.

During one of the breaks, David Gray told me that I had lost Zelinsky early on. Now, I lost Rhee. The only reason we were going on was that Goldstein still understood that I was trying to the best of my ability but growing more confused and more frightened by the moment. Finally, Goldstein threw in the towel, but not until the third day. On Thursday, November 1, 2018, we went until past 6 p.m. I was obviously exhausted, at the point of breaking.

Driving us back to the hotel that night, the two FBI agents gave me a gentle lecture. "Just tell the truth," they instructed me. "When you can't remember, just say you can't remember." These agents were young, and I appreciated their concern. David Gray told me the prosecutors asked the FBI to give me a "pep talk" on the way back to the hotel. Unfortunately, it was not that simple—at least not for me.

On Friday, November 2, 2018, the prosecutors told David Gray my second grand jury appearance had been cancelled, for now. Instead, they let us sleep in by scheduling a pick-up at noon. At breakfast, David Gray was doing everything he could think of doing to keep me out of prison. He wanted to be sure I wasn't letting a mental block stand between me and my simply telling the prosecutors that I was Stone's "source," that I knew Stone was covering-up for me (because supposedly I had contact with Assange) as well as covering-up for him for his "Podesta's time in the barrel" tweet. I was beginning to figure out the prosecutors were pursuing a theory that I was in some kind of conspiracy with Roger Stone, yet I doubted Stone had taken seriously my speculations dating back to August 2016 that I figured out Assange had Podesta's emails.

Right up until the election, I had the distinct impression Stone was fishing everywhere he could to get in touch with Assange. Why would Stone do that if he believed me? Even if Stone had a contact with Assange, perhaps through the journalist James Rosen or thorough the radio host Randy Credico, Stone apparently continued to seek more direct contact for himself. As I have said repeatedly, I do not believe Stone ever met with or spoke to Assange and I couldn't figure out what difference it would have made if he had. Many people interviewed Assange after July 22, 2016, and he never told anyone he had the Podesta emails. Why would Assange tell anyone in advance? That would have ruined the suspense and Assange was a master at using strategically his drops of stolen documents.

On the final day, Friday, November 2, 2016, Rhee, Zelinsky, and Goldstein met privately with David Gray before they came into the windowless conference room to start the Friday interrogation—these long ago quit being mere interviews for me. This was the first time David was unable to walk Mueller's henchmen back off the ledge.

The three stormed into the room, along with their army of FBI agents.

Zelinsky led off with what turned out to be a twenty-minute interview. He was obviously exasperated and angry.

"Doctor Corsi, you live in a different world than we do," he began. "In our world, as lawyers, there are facts. There is also 'true' and 'false.' We are able to distinguish truth from falsity and we do that on the basis of facts. Your world is very different. I have read your books and studied your emails. I have listened to your live chats. You are very skillful at taking a fact from here and a fact from there. Then you weave them together in a lie that you are very good at getting millions of people to believe."

Zelinsky concluded by telling me he thought I had been reduced to the point where I would tell the Special Counsel anything they wanted to hear.

"Write down on a piece of paper what you want me to say, and I will sign it," I answered him, seeing it just made him angrier.

Finally, I thought, Zelinsky is attacking me for the birth certificate. He is claiming that I took a fact from here and a fact from there to weave a narrative that Obama did not have a 1961 Hawaii birth certificate. Obviously, Zelinsky knew this was wrong, because Obama "proved" he had a Hawaii birth certificate when on April 27, 2011, Obama came to the White House press room to release his Hawaii "long-form birth certificate" in a televised press conference. Zelinsky chose to overlook that what Obama released was a computer printout that did not exist in 1961. I wondered if Zelinsky had ever seen the original 1961 birth documents for Obama.

I hadn't seen them, despite years of searching. Zelinsky was not there with me when the Hawaii Department of Health refused to show Obama's original birth documents to Mike Zullo and the other law enforcement members of Sheriff Arpaio's cold case posse. If the Hawaii Department of Health refused to show the original 1961 documents to authorized law enforcement officers conducting an investigation, I wondered how Zelinsky knew Obama was born in Hawaii.

But we were not assembled to debate Obama's birth certificate, even though Zelinsky had just revealed his cards and shown his disdain for me as a right-wing nutcase propagandist. This is the same constantly parroted line that my enemies on the hard left have used to discredit me and ruin my career, ever since the CIA invented the "conspiracy theorist" disinformation tag to discredit anyone daring to challenge the Deep State's ridiculous theory that Lee Harvey Oswald was the lone assassin, killing JFK with a used, worthless Italian-made World War II rifle that was incapable of shooting straight. Ironically, I am writing this on November 22, 2018, the 55th anniversary of JFK's assassination. My world changed the day the Deep State got away with killing Kennedy. Rhee and Zelinsky were not born until after 1963. They were not old enough to have experienced the Vietnam War, or to have appreciated why so many Swift Boat veterans opposed John Kerry when he ran for president in 2004.

I explained to Zelinsky that when I was working my way through college in public relations, my father had hired as a consultant Edward L. Bernays, the father of public relations. "Bernays had a famous phrase," I explained to Zelinsky. "It was 'engineering consent,' and it meant the job of a public relations consultant was to construct facts, so the public could see the value in the proposition or products being advanced by your client. You work in the world of black and white 'facts,' or at least you think you do. Bernays understood the purpose of public relations was to influence public opinion."

When he was giving me his twenty-minute scolding, my mind went to Matthew 18: 37-38. Those verses describe when Jesus, before his crucifixion, was put on trial before Pontius Pilate. Pilate asks Jesus if he is a king. Jesus answers, "Thou sayest that I am a king. To this end I was born, and for this cause came I into the world, that

I should bear witness unto the truth. Every one that is of the truth hearest my voice."

Pilate answers Jesus with a famous question, "And what is truth?"

I have come in my life to accept the Judeo-Christian Bible and Jesus Christ as the truth. Evidently, Pontius Pilate and Zelinsky viewed things differently, that they are arbiters of the truth. For me truth is not relative. Truth derives from God's law, what the ancient Greek philosophers termed "natural law." Every brilliant public relations consultant, starting with Bernays, understood you cannot successfully engineer consent by trying to sell a lie. My problem was that I resolved I would never lie to please Zelinsky, if that's what it took, and as I will demonstrate in the next chapter, I will not lie to sign a fraudulent plea deal Zelinsky has proposed as my only alternative for staying out of prison. If I have to lie, I would rather go to prison.

When Zelinsky was lecturing me, I couldn't help thinking back to my first conversation meeting him—when he explained to me that his grandparents had both escaped Auschwitz. As I mentioned earlier, I have been to Auschwitz twice, and the experiences there changed my life. I came to understand the horror human beings are capable of imposing on other human beings, that "humans are the wolf to humans," as the saying goes. I wondered how Zelinsky's grandparents would feel realizing they survived Auschwitz to produce a grandson who aspired to become the vanguard for Mueller's American version of the Gestapo.

When it came to her turn, Rhee lectured me that I had given them at least four different answers to explain how I knew Assange had Podesta's emails. "You first told us that some man told you. Then you expected us to believe that on an international flight with your wife and family to celebrate your twenty-fifth wedding anniversary in Italy, you had a divine intervention, and that by the grace of God it was magically revealed to you that Assange had Podesta's emails." As she said this, the hate and the scorn were written plain across her otherwise attractive face. I couldn't help thinking back to the see-through blouse, realizing she too lived in a different world than did I. Rhee had made her career defending Hillary Clinton on her emails and representing the Clinton Foundation against charges of racketeering. She was totally uninterested in allowing me to explain why I considered Peter Smith important, in that without Peter Smith, I doubted the NYPD would have found Huma Abedin's emails on Anthony Weiner's laptop.

I realized at that moment that I had become a political prisoner in Mueller's witch hunt. How foolish I had been to think I could assist Mueller reach the truth by turning over my laptops, my Time Machine, my cellphone, my email accounts, my Twitter and Google accounts, and anything else the Special Counsel's office wanted. I had just handed over my whole life, which could be and had been used against me to send me to prison.

Left alone with David after Rhee and Zelinsky stormed out, I asked David if the FBI was going to come in to handcuff me right then to take me to prison.

"Rhee and Zelinsky told me that they had reached a point where all your testimony was useless to them," David explained. "They are even throwing out your grand jury testimony and everything from your first interviews—evidence Rhee told me was absolutely pivotal to their case. They are angry, but they said you can go home for now. Our next step, they said, would be to negotiate a plea deal."

"So that means I am not going to be imprisoned today," I concluded for David. "But I will be imprisoned if I sign a plea deal or if I refuse to sign a plea deal. If I refuse a plea deal, Mueller will just charge me with more severe crimes, calculation I will go to prison after I am convicted at trial."

"That's right," David agreed.

"Will the FBI come to my home to arrest me?" I asked David.

"No, Rhee and Zelinsky said you don't have to be worried about looking out your window to see the FBI in the driveway," David explained. "They said they would work out your arrest with me, after we negotiate a plea deal."

I could see how badly David felt. David had done everything humanly possible. I assured David that he had assisted me greatly by his skill in negotiating with Rhee, Zelinsky, and Goldstein.

I explained to David that I was doomed the minute I realized the prosecutors had a pre-conceived narrative and my answers did not provide them the "facts" they thought they would get from me—facts they thought would pave their way to prosecute Roger Stone successfully and to impeach President Donald Trump.

CHAPTER 12

A Plea Deal to Die For

FRIDAY, NOVEMBER 23, 2018

ON MONDAY, NOVEMBER 12, 2018, I decided it was time to go public about the Mueller affair. I gave my first interview to Christopher Carter of One America News Network (OANN). In that interview, I discussed my two-month psychological harassment at the hands of Mueller's top prosecutors. I also began with my live stream broadcasts on CorsiNation.com to discuss my horror-show experience with Mueller.

In my first interview on OANN, I made public that my inquisition had ended with Mueller telling my lawyer David Gray that my testimony had to be thrown out and that the next stage would be plea negotiations. That meant either I would be indicted for a crime, or I would plead guilty to a crime, but either way I was about to become a felon. The story was getting picked up widely by television, radio, and print media.

The next day, Tuesday, November 13, 2018, I scheduled three in-studio television interviews in New York City: one with Anna Schecter of NBC News, one with Ali Dukakis from ABC News, and the third with NewsMax, the publisher of my bestselling book *Killing the Deep State: The Fight to Save President Trump*. I was planning a massive effort to get the word out about how corrupt and politically motivated the Mueller Special Counsel investigation really was.

To get to New York on Tuesday, NBC sent a limo to bring me from my home in New Jersey to their studio in Rockefeller Center. We had an easy ride across the George Washington Bridge and down the West Side Highway. But going cross-town was a nightmare. We got stuck in a typical New York City gridlock traffic jam. Anna was telephoning nervously to find out where we were. Fighting traffic, we were running late by about a half hour.

The problem was that NBC had reserved a studio and scheduling television time in studio tends to be fairly rigid such that being late creates complications. We ended up having to go uptown, to 57th Street, to beat the cross-town traffic. From 57th Street, we had to turn south along Fifth Avenue to get back to Rockefeller Center. The limo driver was good, but the traffic was horrendous.

Literally, just as the limo driver pulled up to the entrance of the NBC studios at Rockefeller Center on 49th Street, my cellphone rang. It was David Gray.

"Don't do the interview," David insisted. "Have the limo drive you past the NBC studio. Whatever you do, don't stop."

"Why?" I asked, confused. David had helped me set up these interviews, in full agreement that we had nothing to lose by going public.

"Zelinsky, Rhee, and Goldstein just called," David explained. "They are desperate to make sure you stop doing media."

"So what?" I asked.

"They say that they will give you a plea deal," David continued. "You will plead guilty to one minor count. They will say your 'lying' was a mistake. But the important thing is that they will explain to the judge at your sentencing that you deserve no jail time."

I thought quickly about what David said. I hated to leave NBC, ABC, and NewsMax in the lurch at the last minute. But I also hated the idea of being sent to prison, especially for something I did not feel I did. I felt the prosecutors had set a perjury trap that intensified into a nightmare the longer their inquisition carried on. I never intended to lie to Mueller and even today, I am convinced I was attempting to testify to the best of my recollection. The problem was that my recollection of 2016 was not very good, especially when it came to my remembering the details of specific emails and specific conversations, especially without the opportunity to review any of the "evidence" Mueller's prosecutors said they had in their possession.

I made a quick decision and told the driver to continue past the NBC studio entrance, continuing up 49th Street to Fifth Avenue, headed for an undisclosed location, as my attorney had ordered.

"David, you will have to cancel all these interviews," I told him before we ended the call. "It won't be pretty, especially because you won't be able to explain why we have to cancel."

David agreed it would be best if he followed these instructions and cancelled the shows instead of me having to do so.

As he approached Fifth Avenue, the limo driver began sharing with me his life experience.

"You've got to fight Mueller," the limo driver said. "He's just a bully."

During the ride from New Jersey, I had given telephone interviews to Reuters and to a reporter calling from London. Clearly, the limo driver had listened and understood whom he was driving to New York City.

"I'm Jewish," the limo driver continued. "I was raised in a kibbutz. Mueller and these Democrats are crazy. They're all communists."

The driver was emotional about this. "When I was in the Israeli army, I couldn't figure it out. This officer kept bumming cigarettes off me. Finally, I asked him why he didn't buy his own cigarettes. He told me he was still living in a kibbutz and the kibbutz took his salary for the community. The officer said the allowance the kibbutz gave him to live on was not enough for him to afford cigarettes. That's communism. It never works."

The driver was adamant in his advice that I would win if I fought back against the evil Mueller was perpetrating on America. I couldn't believe it. Of all the many limo drivers in New York, this one was my driver today. He was right. I had just published an ebook with three-and-a-half hours of podcasts titled, *Dr. Corsi Investigates: Why the Democratic Party Has Gone Communist.*

After I arrived at the alternative destination, David phoned me again.

"I'm leaving now for Manhattan," he said. "Stay where you are and don't talk to anyone. Don't answer your cellphone unless Monica or I call." David assured me that he had briefed Monica and that she agreed we should go dark again to give Mueller's prosecutors a chance to deliver.

My world was spinning wildly. I ended up in a library where, ironically, I found a copy of Thomas Ricks' book, *Churchill & Orwell: The Fight for Freedom*. The book was about how Winston Churchill and George Orwell, the author of the dystopian novel *1984*, had each worked to fight back totalitarianism in the World War II era.

Through my ordeal with Mueller, I had been rereading Orwell's *1984*. Finding this book at that time seemed to be almost a miracle, as if God was sending me a message to continue the battle against Mueller's role in the Deep State coup d'état against President Trump.

I dived into the book and couldn't put it down. That book also encouraged me, just as the limo driver had encouraged me. The time passed rapidly until David arrived.

That evening, David and I had an early dinner in New York City. I was wound up pretty tight. As we talked it over, we decided we would go dark again, entering into another "no comment" period with the media, until we had a chance to see precisely what plea-bargaining offer Zelinsky, Rhee, and Goldstein would make.

We did not have to wait long. The next day, Wednesday, November 14, 2018, Zelinsky emailed David Gray the plea-bargaining offer. Mueller's henchmen had prepared a one count charge that I had violated 18 U.S.C. Section 1001(a)(2) that specified felony charges for knowingly and willfully making false statements to any agent of the federal government—in my case, specifically the FBI.

The one count charge read as follows:
(False Statements)

On September 10, 2018, defendant JEROME CORSI did willfully and knowingly make materially false, fictitious, and fraudulent statements and representation in a mater within the jurisdiction of the executive branch of the Government of the United States, to wit, the defendant falsely stated and represented to the Special Counsel's Office, including Special Agents of the Federal Bureau of Investigation in Washington, D.C., that he denied an associate's request to get in touch with an organization that he understood to be in possession of stolen emails and other documents pertaining to the 2016 U.S. presidential election, that the associate never asked him to have another person try to get in touch with the organization, and that he did not provide the associate with any information about what materials the organization possessed or what it might do with these materials.

I was incensed reading this. The charges concerned my testimony on the very first day to Rhee, Zelinsky, and Goldstein, and their army of FBI agents that I had not asked Ted Malloch to go see Julian Assange at the request of Roger Stone.

As you will recall from my discussion earlier in this book, the problem with the first day of my testimony was that I had not reloaded from the Time Machine my laptop back to its state on December 31, 2016. I had deleted emails several times just to get the email program to open on that failing laptop. I liked the laptop and Apple had quit making that size laptop. Besides, I wanted to deliver the laptop to the FBI in the state the laptop was in when I quit using it. I did not want to appear to have "sanitized" the laptop by destroying its current state in an effort to reload its 2016 status from the Time Machine.

When I got my laptop back from the FBI, I reloaded 2016 and found the email dated July 25, 2016, in which Roger Stone asked me to "Get to Assange." I had passed that email onto Ted Malloch in London, as I explained earlier. I had totally forgotten about this email, as it turned out I forgot about virtually all my 2016 emails in the intervening time. As you will recall, Mueller's team and the FBI cancelled my first visit to the grand jury that was originally scheduled for Friday, September 7, 2018. The interview with the FBI that blew up over my statement cited in the charge above had occurred on Thursday, September 6, 2018. The date of the charge was wrong. On September 10, 2018, I was back in New Jersey, preparing for the second interview with Mueller and company that was scheduled for Monday, September 17, 2018. Mueller's work here was sloppy, but more importantly it was wrong.

The whole point of giving me until September 17, 2018, was to allow me time to review to the best of my ability the 2016 issues I knew the Special Counsel's office wanted to examine. After David Gray negotiated with Rhee, Zelinsky, and Goldstein, the Special Counsel's office had agreed to allow me to amend my testimony during our next scheduled interview, on September 17, 2018. In my amended testimony, I realized I had passed Roger's message onto Malloch. Also, I found the email chain with Joseph Farah while I was in Italy where I made it clear that if Farah had given me an assignment and bought a ticket to London, I would have gone to see Assange myself.

Now, Rhee, Zelinsky, and Goldstein were charging me with statements they had allowed me to amend. But even more important, even that first day I did not "willfully and knowingly" give them false statements. I had never any idea of trying to deceive Mueller's team. To this day, I would swear under oath that I believe I always told the truth. The problem, as I have tried to make clear in this manuscript, is that my memory of 2016, for whatever reason, is poor. That was abundantly clear to me on September 7, 2016, when I finally got the old, worn-out laptop to reload from the Time Machine its status on December 31, 2016. Clearly, I had forgotten these key emails that the prosecutors had in their possession. My problem throughout was that

Rhee, Zelinsky, and Goldstein pressed me harder and harder to testify on events I truly could not remember. But I still insist that I never "willfully and knowingly" lied.

I was greatly troubled because now, to stay out of prison, Rhee, Zelinsky, and Goldstein under the seal of Mueller's Special Counsel officer were demanding I go before a judge and plead guilty to the above count, which I considered a lie—a lie that Rhee, Zelinsky, and Goldstein knew was a lie. Plea bargaining typically involves a criminal who knows they are a criminal pleading guilty to a lesser charge as a reward for some form of cooperation the prosecutors want. But in my case, the prosecutors were asking me to plead guilty to something I knew I never did. I'm sorry, but I realized immediately I would not "willfully and knowingly" lie by accepting this plea when I knew the count that I was being charged with was a lie. The prosecutors had allowed me to amend my testimony after I restored the 2016 emails (of which there were over sixty-thousand). That was a fact. That was the truth.

Once I accepted this deal and pleaded guilty to this charge in front of a U.S. District Judge, it would be almost impossible to take it back. From that moment on, I would be a federal felon and my life at seventy-two years old would be ruined. Even worse to me, I would have lied in order to stay out of prison. What I decided finally was that I would rather spend the rest of my life in a federal prison than to swear under an oath to God to a criminal charge that I knew in my heart was a lie.

Reading that plea deal, I couldn't help thinking about the several times during my Mueller grilling that I told Andrew Goldstein that I wanted to talk with him about Billy Walters. "I wasn't involved in that case," Goldstein answered me. "But I know you wrote about it."

In 2017, while Goldstein was the chief of the public corruption unit under U.S. Attorney Preet Bharara in the U.S. Attorney's office for the Southern District of New York, Bharara prosecuted William T. Walters, a multi-millionaire investor, Las Vegas-based sports gambler, and philanthropist, with insider trading. Bharara was the same U.S. Attorney who convicted as a felon filmmaker and author Dinesh D'Souza for a relatively minor campaign finance violation. D'Souza was pardoned by President Trump on May 31, 2018.

The federal criminal case for insider trading against noted Las Vegas-based sports gambler William T. "Billy" Walters was seriously impaired in December 2016, when the U.S. District Court Judge P. Kevin Castel in preparing to take the case to trial learned an FBI agent had leaked information on the case to the *New York Times* and the *Wall Street Journal* two years before Walters was indicted.

What the record reveals is, that despite being unable to develop enough evidence to justify a grand jury indictment regarding Walters' trading of either Clorox or Dean Foods stock, Chaves decided in April 2014 that he would prevent the investigation into Walters from going dormant by going to the press and illegally spilling juicy details from the grand jury investigation that he hoped might somehow revive the case.

When Judge Castel understood the extent of Chaves' leaking he demanded U.S. Attorney Bharara must prepare for the court a complete accounting of the FBI leaking activity in the case—a report that Judge Castel subsequently ordered the U.S. Attorney's office to make public in an unsealed and non-redacted form, naming the reporters at the *New York Times* and the *Wall Street Journal* cooperating with Chaves, as well as a full timeline accounting of the numerous leaks both newspapers published.

In Billy Walters appeal, a U.S. Court of Appeals hearing that I attended in a lower Manhattan federal courtroom on Tuesday, May 29, 2018, produced additional evidence to confirm the conclusion that Preet Bharara was guilty of shocking prosecutorial misconduct.

Presiding over the three-judge panel was Judge William Kuntz, from the Eastern District of New York. Just as Assistant U.S. Attorney Brooke E. Cucinella began her argument, Judge Kuntz interrupted.

"FBI Agent Chaves' misconduct in this case was indeed remarkable, wasn't it?" Kuntz asked Cucinella.

"Agent Chaves' conduct in this case was indeed remarkable," Cucinella conceded immediately. "I think that our office's reaction to it at the time was appropriate, and I think that it's something our office and the FBI have taken very seriously and are very disappointed that this has happened.

"It also seems odd that when the issue was raised by the judge the government counsel took a 'Who me?' position. But the government knew a lot," Judge Kuntz interrupted again, his apparent disbelief signaled by the apparently skeptical tone in his voice. "It certainly seems as though Judge Castel would have been on firm ground if he had attacked or questioned the honesty of government counsel."

To that, Cucinella responded, "The government acknowledges we should have done more in the investigation at that point when the allegations were raised. In retrospect, that's something all of us wish had been done."

Again, Kuntz interrupted.

"You speak of allegations," he said skeptically. "At that point the government knew that someone privy to what the grand jury was doing had leaked that information to the newspapers."

Judge Kuntz was right.

In my reporting over the past few years, I have been astounded over the massive Deep State political corruption that began consuming the Department of Justice during the Obama administration. If the U.S. Court of Appeals does not overturn the Walters conviction, President Trump should pardon him.

Now you understand why Goldstein did not want to discuss Billy Walters with me. Goldstein knew that I had the goods on the U.S. Southern District in New York under the political ambitions of U.S. Attorney Preet Bharara—a consuming political ambition that spread prosecutorial corruption to the FBI in New York. I am sure Goldstein understood that I suspected Mueller himself was a Deep State political hack who had shielded the Clintons and the Obamas from justice for decades now. The *Washington Post* noted Goldstein had donated $3,300 to Obama's 2008 and 2012 presidential campaigns.

Reflecting on how he Justice Department under Obama had prosecuted Billy Walters, it made me fume to see the dishonest plea deal that Mueller was offering me. My books and journalistic articles are packed with details that I always heavily reference with copious footnotes. But there I am always working from my research materials and my notes. I am not a human tape recorder where you can press a button and hear back telephone conversations in excruciating detail that I had participated in two years ago.

Being interviewed by Rhee, Zelinsky, and Goldstein, I was grilled for forty hours over two months on material they had as prosecutors that they refused to allow me to see. After Verizon refused to give me my call records for 2016, the only phone call records were the eight pages Zelinsky emailed to David Gray. When those records failed to turn up any "source" to Assange that the prosecutors hoped to find, Rhee, Zelinsky, and Goldstein refused to let me off the hook in my continuing claim I never met or spoke with Assange and I had no "source" who was in contact with Assange.

When David explained the terms Zelinsky had given him for the plea deal, I was outraged.

Mueller's Special Counsel office was insisting that the plea negotiations be completely secret. David instructed me that I was to remain completely silent—that I could not speak to reporters and I would have to discontinue my live stream daily broadcasts on CorsiNation. com. Even when the plea deal was signed, and I went to federal court to plead guilty before a U.S. federal district judge, Mueller's office was demanding that the plea deal would be sealed, completely hidden from public view.

How was this possible in the United States of America? This amounted to Mueller being able to conduct a secret prosecution in a nation where the accused were supposed to be confronted with evidence of their guilt and court proceedings were to be held in the open. I immediately thought of the *Volksgerichtshof*, the "People's Court" in Nazi Germany that was set up as a *Sondergericht*, a "special court" that the Nazis set up outside the constitutional frame of law. In Nazi Germany, this court had jurisdiction over "political crimes," and with Mueller's demands my guilty plea would be secret, I fear the United States is headed in the same direction.

I asked David how long it would be after I pleaded guilty until I was sentenced. He answered that Mueller's Special Counsel planned to delay sentencing.

"How long could Mueller delay sentencing?" I asked.

"Indefinitely," David answered. "Possibly one year, maybe longer."

My outrage mounted realizing the real impact of this plea was to silence me. As a journalist, if I agreed to this plea deal, my First Amendment rights would be stripped. I had to keep my guilty plea a secret and Mueller could keep the conviction secret indefinitely. That meant I had to be silent indefinitely.

"How would I make a living?" I asked David. "What would happen if between pleading guilty and sentencing, I said or did something Mueller didn't like?"

"Mueller only promises to petition the court that you do not deserve jail time at the sentencing hearing," David explained. "If you do anything before sentencing that Mueller doesn't like, the prosecutors are not held to petitioning the sentencing judge for mercy. You could go to jail, even if you take pains to watch what you say or what you do. But you make any slip-up that Mueller doesn't like, and you could still be facing prison time."

This prospect sounded to me like a death warrant. What was clear to me is that Mueller wanted me silenced, out of the way and unable to say or do anything that remotely touched the Special Counselor's witch hunt, or I would be hauled off to prison. Frankly, I might as well be dead, if I signed this agreement. I would have to virtually disappear form the universe—erased like a criminal apprehended by the Thought Police in Orwell's *1984*. How would we pay the monthly bills without me earning an income? We would lose the home we have lived in for over a quarter-century. My credit rating would be devastated, and my ability to borrow money reduced to zero. On ice, like Mueller was proposing, my only real solution would be to go to prison or to kill myself. I knew I couldn't live with Mueller's Sword of Damocles held over my head until he decided to sentence me.

I couldn't believe this was happening to me, especially when I thought about the fact that under Deep State control, justice was no longer blind. In fact, a double standard of unequal justice was the norm of Democrats. When James Comey was FBI Director, Hillary Clinton top aides got immunity deals before talking to the FBI. This included Cheryl Mills, Hillary's long-time attorney and confident, and reach down even to Heather Samuelson, a Clinton staffer-turned-legal assistance who had worked on which State Department emails Hillary planned to designate as personal. Politico reported in 2016 a long-list of Clinton associates who got legal protection from prosecution before talking to the FBI. The list included Bryan Pagliano, the Clinton IT staffer who set up Hillary Clinton's private email server; Platte River Networks engineer Paul Combatta, who erased Hillary's email archives; and John Bentel, a State Department tech staffer who advised subordinates never to discuss Clinton's email server.[47]

I wanted to tell David Gray the only plea deal I would accept would be an agreement by the prosecutors that I would not be prosecuted for anything. That, I knew, was not going to happen yet!

The more I thought about what Mueller was offering, the more I realized it was a terrible deal—really nothing more than a trap. I realized Mueller was so convinced that going to federal prison at seventy-two years old was an unbearable nightmare for me, that he

---

47   Bade, Rachael. "Partisan fireworks over Clinton aides' immunity deals," Politico.com, September 23, 2016. *https://www.politico.com/story/2016/09/cheryl-mills-immunity-deal-reaction-228596.*

calculated to deny me my First Amendment rights as a citizen and as a reporter, to cut me off from earning a living, and to end my book-writing speaking out against the Deep State criminals that I am convinced include Mueller and his prosecutorial henchmen. The Mueller Special Counsel office now appeared to me as a critical part of the continuing treasonous CIA-DOJ Clinton/Obama coup d'état that stunk to high heaven—covering up even a murder at its core.

Why was the criminal investigation into Seth Rich's murder stopped? Simple, because solving that murder would expose that Seth Rich stole the DNC emails, not the Russians. Comey blocked giving immunity to Assange because the Deep State knew Assange could prove Seth Rich stole the DNC emails and got them to WikiLeaks. The basic premise of "Russian Collusion" was a lie—concocted by Hillary and John Podesta, backed up by the CIA and entire corrupt U.S. intelligence apparatus—all designed to frame Donald Trump with a phony Fusion GPS dossier. It stunk. And here I was rapidly becoming a victim of Mueller's criminal activity.

The more I thought about the deal, the less I liked it. I reminded David Gray that I had held securities licenses since the mid-1980s. If I pleaded guilty to a felony, that was a material fact affecting my ability to hold insurance and securities licenses. I reminded David that under federal law, I had an obligation to report all information materially adverse to my ability to hold securities licenses to the Federal Industry Regulatory Authority, commonly known as FINRA. If my plea conviction was sealed, how could I fulfill my reporting obligations under FINRA rules.

"Let me ask the prosecutors," David said.

Zelinsky told David that he was not familiar with FINRA rules. Rhee had the solution. "If the indictment is sealed, then nobody knows and Corsi doesn't have to report to FINRA," she said.

I was astounded to hear this.

"Jeannie Rhee, one of Mueller's top prosecutors, has just advised us to commit a felony," I told David. "The FINRA rules and regulations make no exceptions for sealed indictments or sealed plea deals. I become a federal felon the moment I stand before a U.S. district judge and plead guilty. That's a material fact that affects my ability to hold securities licenses. FINRA does not look kindly on federal felons who try to hide their convictions from FINRA."

I asked David to begin researching ways we could file a complaint in U.S. district court charging Mueller with advising criminal behavior. Just advising me to commit a felony is a felony, I am certain. Mueller just committed another crime and I want to expose it.

Originally, Mueller had only given us one week to consider the deal. When the deal was proposed to David, Mueller gave us only one week to accept it. Mueller had arranged a date on Tuesday, November 20, 2018, for us to appear in federal district court in Washington to plead guilty.

On Thursday and Friday, November 15–16, 2018, New Jersey was hit by a freak early-winter snow storm that paralyzed traffic and made life impossible. David explained to Mueller that there was no way, given his court obligations to other clients and the New Jersey snow storm, that he would have any chance to consult with me in that short time period.

But Mueller was determined to railroad me into a guilty plea. Mueller's team told David Gray that they hand-picked the federal district judge who would hear the case. That judge had agreed to waive the legal formalities to allow David Gray to represent me through the plea hearing and the sentencing, even though David was not admitted to practicing law in Washington, D.C.

This, David told me, would save me about $20,000 because as an alternative, David had arranged for one of his friends, who was an attorney practicing law in Washington, to use his licenses to be admitted to the D.C. bar for this case.

Although Rhee, Zelinsky, and Goldstein were initially resistant to extending the date, they finally agreed to put off the court appearance until late November or early December 2018.

On Wednesday, November 21, 2018, David composed a letter that he planned to send to Mueller.

That letter read as follows:

November 21, 2018
VIA EMAIL
Aaron Zelinsky, Esq.
Office of the Special Counsel

Dear Mr. Zelinsky,

As discussed, Dr. Corsi is still working out the details of the plea agreement with me and we have questions and concerns regarding several categories – 1) not reporting the plea to his broker/dealer as you suggested, 2) the factual allocution, 3) timing/potential bankruptcy filing, and 4) immigrant work visa.

1. *Securities License. Dr. Corsi has a securities license which he will lose as a result of this plea and various FINRA rules regarding disclosure apply to him. I know that Ms. Rhee opined that since this plea would be under seal then Dr. Corsi would not have a duty to report the conviction to his broker/dealer. However, in researching that issue, I think Dr. Corsi cannot keep this secret from his broker/dealer as the law requires him to disclose the plea to his broker/dealer. Dr. Corsi considers the recommendation that he commit a crime to be rather curious—as you represent the Department of Justice. Therefore, if the Office of Special Counsel is requiring Dr. Corsi to refrain from stating anything to his broker/dealer unless and until the plea is unsealed, then I must ask whether your office can provide immunity to him in the event his broker/dealer, or FINRA, raises the issue of failing to report*

the plea agreement to the broker/dealer which is a potential violation of the law.

2. *Allocution. Over the course of six voluntary interviews, Dr. Corsi could not testify that he was ever in touch with WikiLeaks and he could not identify any Russian collusion. He did testify he "wanted nothing to do with Assange/ WikiLeaks." While this is, in a sense true—I understand that this plea to making a false claim is predicated on the fact that Dr. Corsi had emails and phone calls wherein he was in fact interested in WikiLeaks. He had not had the benefit of reviewing all of his emails prior to the interview and you graciously allowed him to review his emails and amend his statements—which he did. Now, after various amendments to his statements, Dr. Corsi is being asked to affirmatively state that he lied to FBI agents. The issue is that the statements that Dr. Corsi made were, in fact, the best he could recall at the time. From the beginning, Dr. Corsi immediately provided all of his computers, emails, phones, social media accounts, etc., and his intent was always to tell you the truth to the best of his recollection, which he admitted to you, was not very good as these events took place years ago.*

3. *Timing of Sentencing/Filing Bankruptcy. I understand that the sentencing would not be scheduled for some time and this plea would hang over Dr. Corsi's head until such time as he is sentenced. During this time, Dr. Corsi would not be able to engage in his live chats or other business dealings as the plea requires his silence. Without this source of revenue and without his securities license, we are looking at a situation in which Dr. Corsi may have to file for bankruptcy—which has a whole other range of difficulties with disclosure. The insistence in having an indefinite period of time between*

plea and sentencing puts Dr. Corsi at risk that some unanticipated event in the interim could be used to change your recommendation for no jail time. I would like to discuss these issues with you before my client can agree to proceed.

4. <u>*Immigration Case*</u>. *Dr. Corsi is currently sponsoring his wife's cousin to come to the U.S. from Argentina on a work visa. I am looking into whether the plea must be disclosed to the immigration authorities in reference to this work visa.*

Please contact me to discuss these issues.
Thank you.

> *Very truly yours,*
> *David E. Gray*
> *Cc: Jerome Corsi, Ph.D.*

The whole plea deal hinged on the willingness of the Special Counsel's office at the time of sentencing—whenever that might happen, or not happen—to petition the court that I should not have to suffer any prison time. But in the statement of charges the Department of Justice sent to David Gray, the Special Counsel noted the maximum penalty under the statute I was being charged with violating involved multiple years in federal prison, several thousand dollars in fines, plus a requirement that under the "sentencing guidelines," the sentencing judge could "impose a fine that is sufficient to pay the federal government the costs of any imprisonment, term of supervised release, and period of probation."

So, if I misbehaved in Mueller's eyes, I could even be required to pay for my own imprisonment, even if imprisonment lasted the rest of my life.

The day after Thanksgiving, David and his family were going on a vacation until Wednesday the following week. I advised David to wait to send the letter to Mueller until he returned. I did not want to be faced with pressure to respond to Mueller until David was back in action.

This is a continuing story, even as I write these pages. What I anticipate will become an issue next is this book. I have written this book in the fear that before I was finished, the FBI would show up at my door, put me in handcuffs, and haul me off to prison in Washington, without even allowing me time to pack a toothbrush or kiss my wife goodbye.

The publisher, Anthony Ziccardi, the founder of Post Hill Press published my book *Obama Nation* in 2008, when he was a VP, Associate Publisher at Simon & Schuster. At Simon & Shuster, Anthony also published my book *America for Sale: Fighting the New World Order, Surviving a Global Depression, and Preserving USA Sovereignty*, in 2009. The next year, 2010, Anthony at Simon & Schuster published my first novel, *The Shroud Codex*, about the Shroud of Turin. Anthony is a trusted friend and we have continued to work together since meeting in 2008.

As soon as this book is listed on Amazon.com—an event that I expect will happen any day now—I expect another firestorm to hit the press.

Today, the day I am writing this last chapter, the *Washington Post* broke the news that I was in plea bargaining with Mueller—a fact that Rhee, Zelinsky, and Goldstein had made clear to David Gray that the Special Counsel's office wanted to remain a secret.

So, as I conclude this last chapter, my life and the future of my family remain on a roller-coaster of emotions—ranging from the fear that I will die in prison to the occasional relief that comes from the unreality that this could be happening in the United States of America. My thoughts on that are reserved for the concluding chapter, "Looking for America." Suffice it to say that today, Friday, November 23, 2018, at seventy-two years old, I never thought I would live to see what is happening to me now happen here.

I conclude by recalling my pride as a child saluting a Veterans' Day Parade in Cleveland, Ohio, as I stood with my parents, with a dad who served in the Army Air Corps and a mother who married him as a young bride when the war was finally ending in Japan. With the Deep State in control of the Justice Department and with Mueller and his henchmen determined to impeach Donald Trump on a false charge of "Russian collusion," those days in America may quickly become a thing of the past.

CONCLUSION

Looking for America

THIS IS NOT the USA!

The hell I went through trying to cooperate with Mueller and intending at all times to tell the truth is not the USA.

Under Mueller, this is the USSA, modeled after the USSR, the Union of Socialist Republics, commonly known as the Soviet Union in Russia.

I have lived seventy-two years and written twenty books since 2004, seven of which were *New York Times* bestsellers, two of which were number one.

I have never been accused of committing a crime in my life, not until I met Mueller.

Now, I am a criminal because I made the stupid mistake of talking to Mueller's prosecutors for forty hours in six grueling sessions over two months.

My crime was that my memory of events in 2016 is not perfect. This I fully admitted, repeatedly.

Mueller's henchmen—Jeannie Rhee, Aaron Zelinsky, and Andrew Goldstein—sat across the table from me and my lawyer, David Gray, determined to quiz me in increasingly granular detail from an eight-inch binder of "files" that contain my emails, my schedules, my published articles, my phone records, and I don't know what else from 2016.

Much of that material I gave them myself when I turned over my computers, my cellphone, my email usernames and passwords, my

Verizon records, my tweets, and my Google account—basically my life in their hands, stripped to the bones.

The binder had my name on it, but as I have noted, Zelinsky refused to answer my question if that binder was all about me. "I won't tell you if this binder is about you, and I won't tell you how many binders like this I have," he insisted.

Over the forty hours, I cannot believe how arrogant these three henchmen and their army of FBI agents are. The prosecutors threw questions at me in rapid-fire fashion. Then they get and angry and belligerent, when my recollection of the truth disagrees with their narrative.

These grand inquisitors, like all grand inquisitors throughout history, insist they only want "the truth." But "the truth" Mueller's grand inquisitors wanted was "the truth" the prosecutors sought from me to fit into their predetermined agenda.

But it is apparent their agenda is to frame Roger Stone for "Russian collusion"—something Hillary Clinton and John Podesta are one-thousand times more guilty of doing than Roger Stone and Donald Trump. But, the real agenda is to impeach President Trump.

But because I have never met or spoken with Julian Assange and because I did not have a contact that passed me information from Assange about the stolen DNC emails in his possession, Rhee, Zelinsky, and Goldstein blow up the interview and threaten to ruin my life.

Amazingly, Rhee, Zelinsky, and Goldstein did not want to hear about the crimes I could document for Hillary Clinton, for John Podesta, for Perkins Coie, for Eric Holder and Loretta Lynch, plus dozens of other Democratic Party officials and their operatives in the CIA, the NSA, and the DOJ, who are still today attempting a traitorous coup d'état against President Trump.

I wrote a *New York Times* bestselling book about that too—it is titled *Killing the Deep State: The Fight to Save President Trump.*

That book is still selling brusquely and the fight to save President Trump is still ongoing. Yet I am the "conspiracy theorist" that Zelinsky claims "lives in a different rule" because I dared to join the Swift Boat veterans in challenging John Kerry's Vietnam War record, because I dared to suggest Barack Obama has a hard left, socialist agenda and lacks the ability to show his original 1961 Hawaiian birth certificate (if such a document even exists).

But my true crime to people like Rhee, Zelinsky, and Goldstein is that I support Donald Trump.

Mueller and company are part of the continuing Deep State coup d'état that seeks to protect Deep State criminals in the CIA and other U.S. intelligence agencies as well as the Department of Justice and FBI.

With this witch hunt predicated on the hoax "Russian collusion" argument, Mueller and company are masquerading as law enforcement agents.

I can attest after my nightmare before with Mueller's Special Counsel office that the USA has become the USSA because I've just experienced the "third degree," lacking only a rubber hose and sleep deprivation to resemble the worst interrogations communists in Stalin's USSR were capable of performing before you were sent to the Gulag to freeze to death working in hard labor.

Make no mistake, Rhee, Zelinsky, and Goldstein are Deep State criminals.

This is what the nation must realize if we have any chance of preserving the freedoms our founding fathers bequeathed us—freedoms countless generations of Americans have fought, bled, and died to preserve—all to be thrown away because the Democrats refuse to investigate themselves.

Sure, Mueller can send me to prison for the rest of my life. He can bankrupt us, ruin our family, and destroy any chance I might have to live my senior years in peace. Mueller can put me in solitary confinement and drive me insane if he so chooses. But I will go to prison protesting my innocence. I did not "willingly and knowingly" provide false information to the FBI, or anyone else.

My memory may not be perfect, but I have based my career on telling inconvenient truths to a growing Deep State establishment that is determined to destroy the Constitution and deny the existence of God, while throwing the nation into a global governance system under which we will lose our sovereignty.

That is what life in the USSA has become.

We all face prison now, if only for thought crimes, if Mueller and company are allowed to rule the land.

Mueller and company could not care that my wife is crying, that CNN had a black SUV parked outside our home bothering us and our neighbors, that our friends are calling hoping that I am able to stay out of prison, destroying the daily peace of thousands.

Mueller and company want us disgraced as a family simply because I could not give Mueller the answers his henchmen keep drilling for in forty hours of their grand inquisition.

But I am the one who has to answer the question, "Is Dad going to prison?"

I have written this book in the belief that there are enough people left in this country who continue to adhere to the constitution and believe in God that Mueller and his Deep State co-conspirators will be stopped before they complete the transformation of the USA into the USSA.

All my life, I have believed that the United States is an exceptional country. I refuse to accept that all those who have fought, bled, and died to preserve our freedoms as Americans will have done so in vain.

In conclusion, I affirm that principle that I strive to live by:
IN THE END, GOD ALWAYS WINS!

I am with God. Are you?